Nine Lives of a Rescuer

By Les Ker

Published by New Generation Publishing in 2014

Copyright © Les Ker 2014

First Edition

The author asserts the moral right under the Copyright, Designs and Patents Act 1988 to be identified as the author of this work.

All Rights reserved. No part of this publication may be reproduced, stored in a retrieval system or transmitted, in any form or by any means without the prior consent of the author, nor be otherwise circulated in any form of binding or cover other than that which it is published and without a similar condition being imposed on the subsequent purchaser.

www.newgeneration-publishing.com

New Generation **Publishing**

The Author asserts the moral right under the Copyright, Designs and Patents Act 1988 to be indentified as the author of the work.

All Rights reserved. No part of this publication may be reproduced, stored in a retrieval system or transmitted, in any form or by any means, electronic, mechanical, photocopying, recording or otherwise, without prior consent of the Author, nor be otherwise circulated in any form of binding or cover other than which it is published and without a similar condition being imposed on the subsequent purchaser.

Whilst every effort has been made that the information given in this book is correct at the time of going to press, no responsibility can be accepted by the Author for any errors or inaccuracies that may appear.

Acknowledgements to:-John Hood who provided flight information and photographs.
Eddie McCallam for information on North Cape Trip.
Great North Air Ambulance Charity.
Royal Air Force.
Andrew Stoddart

This book is dedicated to my Son Jon,
Daughter Fiona, Granddaughters, Rachel, Ellie, Megan
and Poppy.

CONTENTS

Chapter 1: The Plane Crash 7
Chapter 2: The Early Years 13
Chapter 3: Joining the RAF, Lockerbie Air Crash (Bomb Explosion) and Kegworth Airline Crash M1 .. 18
Chapter 4: Fall in the Alps 27
Chapter 5: Bandits in Bolivia (First Accent Cerro Tiquimani South Face) 43
Chapter 6: Paramedic after RAF 56
Chapter 7: Paramedic on Air Ambulance 60
Chapter 8: Flight to Italy in Microlight 69
Chapter 9: Flight to North Cape of Norway (First Person to fly there by Microlight) 72
Chapter 10: Death of friend climbing Ben Nevis (National Bravery Award) 81
Chapter 11: Flight to France in Helicopter 93
Chapter 12: Racing the Orient Express to Istanbul ... 96
Chapter 13: Recovery after Air Crash 101
Chapter 14: Rocket Attack Iraq 108
Chapter 15: Held at Gunpoint Iran 111
Chapter 16: Life Goes On 113

Chapter 1: The Plane Crash

It was a fine day with the sun shining and a few clouds floating across the sky. Jon rang his mate Jim Martin and suggested they went for a flight in their Bambi microlight aircraft. The date was the 30th December 2007 and possibly the last time they would be able to do some flying before the bad weather set in. They decided to fly over to Carlisle Airport for the day but first they would call at Eshott Airfield and see who was there.

The Bambi was stored in the hangar at Eddie's grassed airfield near Longframlington. They both decided to wear the same type of clothes, flat cap and country style clothes. Arriving at the airfield about eleven o'clock, they pulled the Bambi out of the hangar and went through the usual checks to make sure everything was working correctly.

They started the engine and taxied out onto the grassed runway. The Bambi was a fixed wing microlight plane with a strong Perspex canopy which covered the cockpit. Its powerful little engine soon had them in the air and they climbed quickly to about a thousand feet. They headed towards Eshott Airfield staying around the thousand feet mark showing on the controls. Jon was flying the plane as they moved across Burgham Golf course near Felton, when suddenly there was a juddering at the back of the plane and the tail piece sheared off. The plane immediately started to dive head first towards the ground.

Jim shouted out "Jon I've got the controls."

He struggled with the joy stick and pedals but managed to head the aircraft towards some trees at the edge of a fairway on the golf course. There was a small stream running alongside the trees and as the plane crashed into them, it came to rest nose first in the soft ground next to the stream.

The front end was now deep into the ground and the canopy was smashed, as the two pilots heads had crashed into it. The reason for this was because the seatbelts had broken away from their moorings in the cockpit and both pilots heads had been flung forward into it.

On the golf course there were four golfers playing a round of golf and they saw all this happen and immediately called the emergency services for help.

Both pilots had been knocked out at this stage and as the ambulance arrived, the medics realised that both airmen were badly injured. "Corky", one of the medics, recognised both men. Jim was a Great North Air Ambulance Pilot and Jon was one of the Senior Paramedics with them, who flew with Jim on a regular basis.

The Fire Brigade had now arrived and came to assist with getting the airmen out of the crashed plane. Jon was now conscious at this point but very confused and agitated, indicating that he had a serious head injury. Jim was unconscious and having difficulty breathing with head and facial injuries. It also appeared that both men had severe leg injuries.

Suddenly the Senior Fire Officer called out, "Everyone clear the scene now."

"Corky" piped up, "These are our friends and colleagues we need to get them out."

The Fire Officer replied, "The instrument panel is sparking and with all this aviation fuel we need to move away to safety."

"Corky" leaned across into the cockpit and ripped the panel out and threw it into the stream, "There, it's not sparking now, can we have some help to get our injured colleagues out."

By now the Great North Air Ambulance and the Police Helicopter were on the scene and everyone worked hard to free the pilots. Jim was placed in the Air Ambulance and Jon, who was still conscious, was put into the Police Helicopter and both were taken to the Newcastle General Hospital.

The crash teams at Newcastle General Hospital were now ready for the incoming helicopters. The pilots, Jon and Jim, were taken straight into Intensive Care and their treatment started.

Barbara, Jon's partner, was at work and it was now about four hours after the accident. Suddenly she got a telephone call from her daughter Hannah.

Hannah said, "Mam, tell me Jon isn't out flying in his plane?"

Barbara replied, "Why?"

Hannah came back with, "It's just been on the radio that there's been a crash of a light aircraft on a golf course near Felton."

Barbara replied, "I haven't heard anything but I'll ring John Hood as he'll know about it. I'll ring you back."

Barbara rang John and asked him, "John have you heard about the air crash near Felton, do you know who it is, Jon and Jim are out flying?"

John replied, "Barbara haven't you been told it's Jon and Jim and they are both in Newcastle General seriously injured."

She now needed to get away from work so she could go to the hospital. This was no problem and she rushed home to get changed. She got her things together and then rang Jon's parents, Maureen and Les, to tell them what had happened.

She then set off, with Hannah, to Newcastle General Hospital to see him. When she arrived she was told by staff that both men were in theatre being operated on.

Maureen and Les, who fortunately had been at home when Barbara rang, started to get ready to travel to Newcastle from their home in Guisborough. Barbara had not heard anything from the Police about the accident so Les rang Northumbria Police for more information on the accident and asked why Barbara hadn't been informed.

The Liaison Inspector rang back and advised us all about the accident. He also stated that there was no rush to get to the Hospital as both pilots were still in theatre undergoing operations on their injuries. Maureen and Les set off for Newcastle wondering what the news was going to be regarding their Son's and Jim's injuries.

The journey seemed long and not much was said, both parents with their own thoughts as they approached the Newcastle General Hospital. They parked up and made their way to the Accident and Emergency Department. As they made their way down the long corridor towards the Intensive Care area, they could hear voices in a room and there found Barbara, Hannah, Margaret (Jim's wife) and her friends. Introductions were made by Babs and then she updated Maureen and Les of the current situation.

The position was that both men were still in theatre and would be for some time, as the Surgeons worked on the extensive injuries the pair had received. It was a miracle they were still alive and prayers were privately being said for their survival. It was now early evening but a long wait was ahead for the worried partners, family and friends.

The chat was very general as the time dragged by and food was collected in the form of sandwiches. Although not that hungry the group ate as they waited for news. Anxiety was now showing on everyone's face.

It was now the early hours of the morning and suddenly the Consultant appeared and started to explain to the different parties the extent of the injuries. Jon's most serious injury was the massive bleed which had formed behind the right side of his forehead. The Consultant at this stage could not even say he would come out of the coma because it was such a large bleed and if it didn't stop and disperse the brain would be badly damaged.

He also explained that they had repaired his broken left femur by putting a titanium rod inside the bone to stabilise the thigh. The outside of Jon's right ankle was shattered but they had managed to put a plate in and screw all the bones back together. There was one problem with the injury, in that the skin had all been torn away so he would need a skin graft, sooner rather than later, to repair and cover the damaged bone to prevent infection.

Jon's partner Babs and Parents were now allowed to go into the Intensive Care Ward and see him. It was a shock to see him wired up to all the machines and his chest rising and falling as the air was put in automatically. There was no movement other than that as they watched the almost lifeless body.

The Consultant stated, "If the bleed in his brain stopped and the clot started to disperse they would gradually bring him out of the coma."

They left the ward after some time feeling helpless because they couldn't do anything. They could only pray and leave it all in God's hands as to whether either of the pilots were going to make it through this critical time.

Was this the end, had Jon ran out of those nine lives. We need to go back and look at his life, the near misses, the rescues, the exciting and dangerous adventures he had done in his short 44 years.

Paramedics and Firemen working to free Jon and Jim from the crashed Microlight Bambi

Chapter 2: The Early Years

It was Father's day June 1969 and in the early hours of the morning a baby boy of eight pounds was born to Maureen and Les. This bundle of joy was always active and this proved to be the way he would be throughout his life. Christened Jonathan Leslie he later became known as Jon Ker.

As he started to crawl and get about something happened one morning that pointed to his future activities. Once awake, like all children, he soon let us know he needed some attention. This particular morning he made the usual noise shouting for us. He then went silent and suddenly there was an almighty crash and I rushed into his room to see what had happened. There, sat on the floor, was Jon with a great big grin on his face. He was saying without any words, look at me Dad I got out all on my own. I checked the cot straight away and found it was all intact. The only way he could have got out of it was to climb over the side. This was the first indication that he was going to be a climber and was prepared to take risks.

He was soon walking about and getting into everything he shouldn't, as kids do. At this time we lived in Ormesby but when the opportunity arose we moved back to Guisborough before Jon's second birthday.

It was in this new house, shortly after we had moved in, that his first near miss experience happened. Jon had gone into his bed for his usual afternoon nap and we saw the chance to get on and sort the garden out. After a short while Maureen said "I'll go and check to see if Jonathan is awake."

Suddenly I heard Maureen shouting from inside the house and I rushed in to find her sitting on the stairs, shaking all over with Jon in her arms. She explained, he was stood at his gate choking and was blue in the face. I picked him up, hit him on the back and a marble fell out of his mouth.

How Jon had got hold of this single marble we'll never know as we had no marbles in the house. If Maureen had not gone to check on him he may have died.

As Jon grew up he loved to be active and he became a very good walker as well as getting involved in different sports. He became a good swimmer and achieved all the swimming awards he took.

We had moved again, our house was now right on the edge of the Guisborough forest. In the field next to our house was a large oak tree and when he was big enough Jon would climb it at every opportunity. We didn't know about this until one day he had persuaded his cousin Andrew to climb the tree with him.

I was in the house at the time when I heard shouting, "Dad Andrew's stuck in the tree."

I went outside to find Andrew clinging to the second branch up unable to move. He was literally frozen on the oak. Jon was right at the top as high as he could go.

I shouted, "Jonathan come down from there and help me get Andrew down."

It took me quite a time as I coaxed Andrew, bit by bit, down the tree. Jon thought it was really funny but Andrew didn't go climbing again for a long time.

He was now at senior school and soon showed his fitness by winning the first year cross country race very easily. He went on to win every cross country race right through each year until leaving the school and going to college.

It was at the end of his first year in senior school that we went on holiday to Scotland. We had a caravan by now and were staying at a Caravan Park near to Fort William. It was wet most of the time we were there. However we did have a couple of good days when it didn't rain and it was on one of these days Jon and I decided to climb Ben Nevis. I had climbed the Ben way back in 1963 and was looking forward to the challenge again. It was Jon's first experience climbing a big dangerous mountain. We were wearing all the right gear which proved to be of value when we got to the top. It took us just under two and half hours to reach the summit and although it was the middle of August it was snowing on the top with the visibility down to about 30 metres. We had set off up the well trodden path in fine weather, but it changed very quickly and it was cold as we neared the summit. We had our food in the hut at the top of the "Ben" and then set off down. This was Jon's first big climb and he loved it. Later in his life he would return many times to Ben Nevis, climbing the sheer cliff faces, on the North side, in both summer and winter.

It was about this time that he started to free climb around the Guisborough area. I only found this out because he let slip that one of his teachers, who was a mountaineer, showed him how to climb round the old railway bridges. He also admitted to climbing Highcliffe Nab without any ropes for security. We decided, at some cost, to send him on a specialist course, to learn correctly, how to climb and keep safe.

I got into climbing through a work colleague who had climbed with a well known climber, so as soon as his course had finished Jon and I went climbing on the local hills near to Guisborough. He was a very good climber and now I could see he was very safe in the way he set up his equipment. He left school and gained a place on the Sports Science Course at the college in

Middlesbrough. The first year there was just up his street, lots of sporting activities and awards to gain. His swimming and life saving ability was soon acknowledged by the tutor and he was her star pupil. This helped him obtain a lifeguard job through the summer period, which he thoroughly enjoyed, driving the rubber dinghy about on the rough sea.

One day he was jumping the waves when the boat threw him out and he was left in the water watching it go round and round in a large looping circle. He had to stay in the water until it ran out of petrol before he could climb back aboard and row it to shore which, by this time, was about half a mile away.

During the college year all the students had the chance of some work experience, normally one of their own choice. Jon picked a trip to the Lake District working at an Outdoor Centre near Windermere. He spent four weeks there and we went over to see him half way through when he had been given a day off.

I went climbing with him while his mother spent time reading. We went to Shepherd's Crag and he decided we would climb Ardus which is a two pitch ascent. I was a bit concerned because I wasn't as good a climber as him but I went along with it. We soon got to the first pitch and then I watched Jon traverse left across the rock which had only a few small hand holds. He then moved up with ease and put another bolt into the rock to keep himself safe in case he fell off. I allowed the rope to feed out and he soon reached the top of the climb. He secured himself and the rope giving me the all clear to climb. I was concerned at the traverse as I was leaving the safety of the ledge.

I shouted up to Jon, "Keep the rope tight son so it gives me some confidence."

"OK, Yes I'll keep it tight." he replied

I then set off across the rock face. As I got to the point to move up, I saw there were only two small handholds just large enough to get two of my fingers on each of them. The rope had gone a little slack on the traverse out and I shouted for Jon to tighten it up. There was no reply. Knowing there was a long drop beneath me, adrenalin pumping, I went for the move, pulling with my arms and pushing up with my legs, I grabbed the big jug above me and then steadily made my way to the top of the climb.

When I got there I said to Jon, "Didn't you hear me shouting for you to tighten the rope."

He replied, " Sorry, I've just been talking to a famous mountaineer about climbing."

What could I say, the great iconic climber had gone and missed my epic ascent.

Jon had really enjoyed his work experience and talked our heads off about it when he returned home.

We continued to climb different crags in the North Yorkshire area during the rest of his first year at the college. He was now ready to decide on his second year but because it was going to be more academic and less physical he didn't want to do it.

We had discussions with him for quite a while, making sure he would make the right decision as to which job he chose.

Chapter 3: Joining the RAF, Lockerbie Air Crash (Bomb Explosion) and Kegworth Airline Crash M1

Jon ultimately made up his mind deciding to join the Royal Air Force (RAF). He applied at the local office in Middlesbrough and was accepted as a Motor Transport driver. Car mad, he was learning to drive at the time and he couldn't wait to pass his test. The Royal Air Force would train him and put him through his test once he had done his basic training.

He was soon off on his basic training which for him was held at Hereford. On the physical side of the course Jon showed how good his fitness levels were by excelling in all aspects of it. At the end of his training he received an award for all the effort he had put into the physical side.

The next part of his training was held at St Athan in South Wales. In no time he had completed all his driver training, passing his test at the first go and was then posted to RAF Boulmer in Northumberland. This station was situated next to the small village of Longhoughton, where Jon was billeted in one of the RAF houses. The isolation of the base meant he needed a car to get to work and to travel home. With our help he bought a Vauxhall Chevette which looked and drove really well. He was now able to get home on his days off and keep in touch with his friends from the rock group they had formed when he was at school and college.

It was on one of the trips home when his next near miss happened. It was December and the snow was falling quite quickly laying a thick carpet on the paths and roads. I advised him to set off early back to

Longhoughton so he was travelling in the daylight. The temperature had dropped to well below freezing and the roads were treacherous.

When Jon entered Northumberland on the A1, he noticed the roads were getting extremely icy as he travelled north. He was on a downhill part of the road, when suddenly he lost control and the Chevette veered left, mounting the kerb and up the steep embankment at the roadside. As it climbed the snow covered steep grass slope, unexpectedly it turned over onto its roof and slid down towards the tarmac. Jon reacted instantly, throwing himself across the two front seats, which saved his life, because the roof was crushed flat to the steering wheel. He eventually managed to get out of the car via the rear window and had only a few scratches to his name.

He was also lucky that a passing vehicle had seen what had happened and gave him a lift to his destination at Longhoughton.

Over the next few months he travelled miles up and down the country completing deliveries and transporting the hierarchy to their important meetings. It was on one of these latter assignments that Jon's First Aid skills came to light.

He had taken the Squadron Leader to a meeting in Wales and they were travelling along the A1, returning to RAF Boulmer, when an accident took place right in front of them. Jon calmly put all the hazard warning lights on the vehicle and went to help the injured parties in the crash. The Squadron Leader had contacted the emergency services and then went over to assist. Jon continued to treat the injured until the ambulance arrived, then handed it all over with a full description of what he had done.

The Squadron Leader was so impressed, he made a special report on his return to the camp, a commendation of his actions was recorded and placed on Jon's personal file.

Being at Boulmer he was next to the RAF Rescue Helicopter pad and was soon chatting to the pilots and winch-men, finding out about their training rescues. It was during one of these chats that he volunteered himself to be a casualty in a practice sea rescue.

He was kitted out in a dry suit and they would drop him into the sea then carry out the rescue. On board, fully dressed for the rescue, the helicopter took off and headed out to sea. It had climbed to about 500 feet and was just over the sea when the pilot switched everything off.

In Jon's words, "It fell like a stone for about 100 feet before the pilot switched everything back on. My stomach came up into my mouth. "

This was the initiation to his helicopter ride. They then headed out to sea and about a mile out they dropped Jon into the water and then flew off.

Jon said, "I was in the water for ages I reckon about 20 minutes before I saw the yellow helicopter coming back to get me out. It was a great relief and I was soon back on board in the warm."

He was enjoying his time at Longhoughton gaining a lot of driving experience in different types of vehicles.

We continued to climb the cliff faces at Guisborough, Wainstones and Kildale in North Yorkshire when he was home. We also started climbing at Corby's Crags in Northumberland which are between Alnwick and Rothbury and although not very high, there were some good climbs on it. It was on these crags that he had another lucky escape. He was climbing the route called "Audacity" with his girlfriend acting as support with the rope. He was about 20 feet from the ground when he slipped off. Instead of locking the rope off on the plate, his girlfriend grabbed at the rope which slid straight through her hands burning them badly and skinning part of one hand to the bone. Jon landed quite heavily and broke his 5th metatarsal in his right foot. It could have been worse but meant he was only five weeks out of action.

It was during this time that Jon saw an internal memo asking for volunteers to take part in trials to become part of the RAF Mountain Rescue Section. Fit once more he requested a place on the forthcoming trial and was accepted, although he was only 18 years old at the time.

The trial was based in Scotland with Sergeant Dave (Heavy) Whalley from the RAF Lucas Mountain Rescue Team in charge of the assessments. The candidates had to demonstrate their abilities and skills whilst walking and climbing throughout the Grampian Mountains. Jon really enjoyed the challenge and soon displayed his excellent fitness levels and very good rock climbing skills. After walking through Glen Coe on one of the days they reached the base of Ben Nevis. This time they were at the foot of Tower Ridge, which is one of the rock faces and goes straight up two thousand feet to the summit.

Jon explained, "It was a daunting task. I'd never been up anything like this before and the step across the gap, near the top, was really scary. But I did it and felt chuffed about it."

Looking down Tower Ridge from the top of Ben Nevis
You can see the Tower Gap near to centre left of picture

They then went across to Isle of Skye but the weather closed in and they were not able to do the climbs that were planned in the Cuillin hills. Needless to say, although only eighteen, he passed the trial with flying colours.

As Jon related afterwards, "Heavy" later said to me, "You were never a trialist Jon, watching you climb that E2/3 at Dunkeld, after a full day on the mountains was awesome. You had all the attributes to be part of the Mountain Rescue Section."

He would now wait for a vacancy becoming available in one of the teams which are based all around the United Kingdom.

It wasn't long before he was called to visit RAF Linton-on-Ouse where the Northern Mountain Rescue Team were based. He spent some time with the team and with having such a good report from his trial they welcomed him on board. He moved into Linton-on-Ouse and he was soon walking the fells and mountains all around the Lake District getting to know the terrain which would help him during rescues.

One of his earliest visits was to the crash site of a fighter plane which had flown into the mountainside. Unfortunately there were no suvivors.

With his new colleagues Jon was soon rescuing the injured from the hills and mountains in the Lake District. Sometimes they had to call on the Sea King helicopter at RAF Boulmer to assist with these rescues. He knew all the pilots and winch-men, which helped in the working relationship.

Young Jon relaxing at the new Mountain Rescue Unit at RAF Leeming

It was now into December 1988 and the RAF Mountain Rescue Team were moving to RAF Leeming where a new building had been built for all their modern equipment. On Wednesday 21st December they decided to have a party at the new centre at RAF Leeming which they had just moved into. The party was going well and everyone was having a good time. The telephone suddenly started ringing and the

Sergeant, Leader of the team, eventually went over to answer it.

The voice on the other end of the phone said, "There's been an aircraft crash at Lockerbie can you get a team together."

The Sergeant replied, "You are kidding! You know we are having a party over here, bye."

As he started to leave the office, the phone rang again, he answered it to hear, "Sergeant this is not a joke there has been an air crash and the plane has come down on Lockerbie. A Chinook helicopter is on its way to pick you and your team up and transport you to the site to search for the bodies and wreckage."

He informed his team of the emergency and they were soon putting all the gear together, ready for their flight to Lockerbie in southern Scotland. The Chinook soon arrived and they were on their way north west to Lockerbie. As they arrived, the large fire in the village stood out against the dark ground. They landed and every member, including Jon, were given their task and markers for any bodies they found. Sergeant Dave (Heavy) Whalley, who was in charge of the operation, gave them the information about the spread of the Boeing 747 wreckage, which indicated a bomb blast on board.

As Jon searched for wreckage and bodies, he was soon finding them.

He then found part of the fuselage and reported it. The reply came straight back, don't move from there and don't let anyone near it. Within about a couple of minutes an American helicopter was on site, they took the black box from the wreckage he had found and without saying a word they just flew off.

The next three days Jon and the team had hardly any sleep as they searched for bodies, property and wreckage, making sure they had covered all the terrain it was scattered over. This was no doubt a traumatic time for them all, especially Jon who was only 19 years old. Two hundred and fifty nine people from the aeroplane were killed in the worst air explosion in the United Kingdom.

Finally they were stood down and headed home. I picked Jon up from Linton-on-Ouse in the late evening and he talked my head off as we made our way home to Guisborough. He continued to chat on, late into the night, about the devastation that had happened in Lockerbie. It certainly had had an effect on his emotions during that stressful time searching and finding all those bodies. He then slept for nearly twenty four hours catching up on his sleep.

After a couple of days, we took him back to camp as he was due to go with the team to the Lake District for more training and cover any incidents that may occur.

Christmas soon came and went and on Sunday 8th January the team were returning from the Lake District when they got a call to attend another air crash which had happened on the M1 next to the village of Kegworth. A large Airliner had come down while approaching the West Midlands Airport.

They were the second team to arrive at the scene.

In Jon's words, "It was utter chaos because there were so many people just driving to the scene to see what had happened, making it almost impossible for us to get through to help with the rescue."

When we finally got there most of the injured were out of the aeroplane and had been taken to hospital. Sadly forty seven people lost their lives in that ill fated crash.

Again Jon had been in the thick of the action during this rescue and on return to their unit at RAF Leeming, all the team were offered counselling because of the two serious incidents they had attended, but they all declined.

Chapter 4: Fall in the Alps

He was now well and truly part of a very good Mountain Rescue Team. They trained every day practising their rescue skills and advanced first aid treatment on site at Leeming, as well as the specialist courses at local hospitals. Each weekend the team would cover the Lake District National Park and this is when they would develop their ability to rescue injured persons from the Cumbrian Mountains and Fells. The terrain and the quick change of weather makes it a very dangerous place to train but the team's fitness and dedication allowed them to cope adequately.

Their next real search occurred when a freak air crash happened just above the mountains of Borrowdale. A Jaguar fighter plane and a Tornado jet collided in mid-air. The Tornado, which had been climbing out of the valley was now flying upside down after the collision. The pilots ejected even though they were facing the ground. They were lucky because their seats righted themselves and they parachuted to safety, landing in nearby woods. As Jon and the team made their search for the wrecked Jaguar, the Fire Brigade arrived, to be met by the two pilots who confirmed who they were and what had happened. They only had a few minor injuries after such a crash and walked unaided out of the woods. They secured the area until the crash site team and investigators arrived to conduct their findings.

That wasn't the only Jaguar crash site Jon attended during his time in the Mountain Rescue. The other one was at the cliffs in Coldingham Bay, Northumberland. It appears the pilot had not pulled the plane up soon enough before colliding with the cliffs. This was a difficult recovery operation as Jon and the Mountain

Rescue Team had to help the crash site team down the cliffs. This was achieved by abseiling them down the steep sea cliffs. The Mountain Rescue Team had to stay and help with the rescue and what wreckage they could recover. A Puma helicopter arrived during this time and recovered the engine from the Jaguar which had ended up on the beach. It was quite a long operation lifting the engine from the sand and the pilot of the Puma wasn't very happy when some of the other jets, who were up flying that day, kept passing over the site to see what had happened.

Another call they received was to Great End, near Scafell Pike, where an ice climber had fallen and his companions stated he was badly hurt. On arrival they found the guy at the bottom of a gully, but sadly there was nothing they could do for him. The terrain with the snow and ice on the ground made it impossible to carry out the rescue successfully, so the RAF Sea King was requested.

The next incident required them to go onto the A66 at Brough because there were numerous cars stuck in the snow between Brough and Bowes on the Pennines. Jon and the team had to travel from Great End, where they had been training, so it was some time before they reached the A66. The roads were really deep in snow but the Land Rover Defender made fairly easy work of the conditions. When they got to Brough the snow was a lot deeper and it was time to put boots and snow shoes on. The cars, which had been abandoned on the A66, were now covered up to the roofs in snow. The instructions from the Police were to check that no one was still inside any of the vehicles. It was thirteen miles to Bowes and every car was checked as the team made their way there. Fortunately all the cars were found to be empty of their drivers and passengers. The team spent the night at the Bowes Moor Inn together with a host of occupants of the cars which had been abandoned because of the snow. The RAF Sea King rescue helicopter had also been called out and had to land at the Bowes Moor Inn because of the freezing weather conditions. The rotor blades were all iced up so they also had to stay the night at the hotel. The next morning the weather was much better and the drivers/occupants made their arrangements to get home as the snow ploughs reopened the roads. The ice was removed from the rotor blades and the Sea King was soon airborne again. Jon and members of the team, who had accomplished the searches, were in luck as the Sea King dropped them off at Leeming before making its way back to RAF Boulmer.

The dangers of sudden and heavy snow falls in Great Britain is a major problem especially for the Mountain Rescue Teams. So the importance of training in winter snow conditions had to be comprehensively achieved in some depth. This meant the team would travel to the Alps in Europe and develop their knowledge in snow and ice climbing. They would also learn about avalanches and how they are created and the dangers of crossing terrain where one could be triggered off by the slightest sound or movement.

Jon's sense of adventure was heightened by these visits to the Alps but it was also another place where he had a scrape with death.

The thrill of climbing Mont Blanc, Europe's highest mountain at 4,810 metres (15,781feet), was just the start. He then went on to climb the Matterhorn from the Italian side followed by the north face of the Eiger. Jon also climbed Grandes Jarasses, Aiguille Verte, Aiguille du Midi, Aiguille du Chardonnet, Croz Spur and Aiguille de L'm. All the mountains, except for

Aiguille de L'm 2,844 metres (9,461feet), were around 4,000 metres (13,125feet) above sea level with some stunning views of the Mont Blanc Massif.

Jon lead climbing an Ice wall on Petit Verte on the Mont Blanc Massif

Jon resting after reaching the Summit of Mont Blanc

The Matterhorn in Switzerland

The North Face of the Eiger in Switzerland

As Jon said, "Mont Blanc was just a stroll when you consider what is involved climbing the Matterhorn and Eiger. The Matterhorn's main danger is rock falls, as the temperature rises in the morning, they become a major hazard if you are still on the mountain. That's why you start climbing in the middle of the night so that you are off the mountain before mid-day."

He then went on to explain how hard the North Face of the Eiger was to climb. Again rock and ice breaking off the sheer face is a worry but he managed it safely.

In 1990 during another visit to Chamonix in France Jon climbed Mont Blanc once again, finding it much easier this time. It was during this visit that his mate saw an advert in a shop for some clothing and said, "That's you Jon!! You'll now be known as Jonny Munster." The nickname stuck and even after he had left the RAF he was still known to all the team members as "Jonny Munster".

The next day, with a friend from the St. Athens team, he decided to climb Aguille-Du-Midi which is next to Mont Blanc. It is over 12,500 feet high and has a cable car which takes you to the top. On a clear day you can see the Matterhorn as well as all the French,

Swiss and Italian Alps. There is also a cable car which travels onto Mont Blanc.

The weather was pretty good when they set off and were soon over halfway up the mountain. Like all mountainous regions the change in weather conditions can alter very quickly and suddenly they could see an electric storm heading their way. Jon made the decision to get off the Aguille-Du-Midi as soon as possible. They started to abseil off the mountain when the freak accident occurred. His companion had just got off the rope and Jon started to abseil down to him at the next point, when the lightning struck the rocks above him and broke away some large chunks, which came tumbling down the mountain. Some of these rocks sliced through the rope and Jon was now falling down the mountain. His friend had the presence of mind to wrap the bottom end of the rope round a rock, which he was stood next to. This action probably saved Jon's life as it slowed his fall.

Jon stated to me later, "I knew I was in trouble and I had to keep conscious to see if I could stop the downward momentum. The rope suddenly slowed me as I tried to keep in a ball and I managed to lodge myself on a small ledge. Below was a 1,000 foot drop which I wouldn't have survived. I was pretty badly injured but still conscious. I couldn't straighten my elbow and one of my knees had been badly cut and damaged where the rocks had pierced it . The helmet I was wearing was smashed to pulp, I think it saved my skull from serious harm. I fell about 200 feet."

As the storm had started Jon's Sergeant had been watching them abseiling down through the binoculars and saw the fall. He immediately called out the rescue helicopter which winched the injured Jon and his friend off the mountain.

Jon was taken to the local hospital where he was diagnosed with having compression of the brain. His other injuries were treated and he was discharged.

The team had travelled out to Chamonix in a Sherpa van but Jon was in no state to make that journey back to the UK. After some negotiating, he was transported by air to the RAF hospital at RAF Wroughton where he spent the next two weeks recovering from his accident.

His arm and knee soon healed but his brain damage took a little bit longer and it was over a year before the pupils in his eyes were back to normal. This apparently is a common thing with severe compression.

After a couple of months Jon was back out, with the team, training and climbing again. I also went out climbing with him and at first, I noticed he had lost some of his confidence when the climb was getting hard. It only went on for a few months and he was back clearly climbing as good as ever.

This was apparent when Jon and a colleague climbed all four ridges on the North face of Ben Nevis, in one day. They went up the North East Buttress, down Tower Ridge, up Observatory Ridge and finally down Castle Ridge. David (Heavy) Whalley met Jon while he was descending Tower Ridge and couldn't believe what he was doing that day. Regular climbers will know this is some feat in one day.

Jon told me, "We mainly climbed without ropes otherwise we wouldn't have had time to do all the ridges. "Heavy" was in disbelief at what we were doing as we passed him on Tower Ridge."

Jon loved climbing Ben Nevis and Glen Coe and on his time off you would see him head north to Fort William and climb his favourite mountain. His knowledge of this area would save the lives of two climbers.

It all started when the RAF Mountain Rescue Team, based at Leeming, were asked to cover the Scottish Mountains while the normal team from the area were given a rest. The RAF Lossimouth Team had been in the mountains for three weeks solid, because of irresponsible people going out on the mountains ill equipped and getting into trouble in the snow.

The team had been at Fort William for a few days when the weather became worse and heavy snow started falling. A report came in about 7pm, stating two climbers from London had not returned as expected. Their route was to climb the Aonach Eagach Ridge, then onto Clachaig Gully in Glen Coe finishing at Clachaig Hotel about 5pm.

The weather had deteriorated rapidly during the afternoon but even in these atrocious conditions Jon and a colleague went out to see if they could find them.

As Jon said to me later, "Dad, we shouldn't have been out there in a near blizzard but if we didn't find them there was a chance they would die in Glen Coe from exposure."

Jon and his colleague were soon on the Aonach Eagach Ridge and as they got to the point called "The Chancellor", there huddled together, were the two missing climbers. Apparently as they reached this point on the mountain, they became disorientated and had become rooted to the spot, not being able to go forward or back. Fortunately their clothing was top quality which had protected them from the severe elements.

They were capable of walking off the mountain, so Jon and his colleague roped them up and they all set off up the ridge. This was the safest way to get out of the snow covered Glen Coe and they were soon descending down Clachaig Gully and managed to reach the

Clachaig Hotel before it closed. The two climbers were very grateful and had learnt an important lesson about tackling Aonach Eagach Ridge in poor weather conditions.

Glen Coe with Aonach Eagach Ridge centre of picture.

Aonach Eagach Ridge, Glen Coe

The next week a single mountaineer went missing on Ben Nevis. He had been climbing the North Face of the mountain but had not returned as expected. Jon, together with the local Mountain Rescue Team, spent the weekend searching for him but to no avail.

The local team had to leave after the weekend but the RAF team continued the search. Again they searched the North Face of Ben Nevis.

Jon said, "As we searched the climbing area again, we suddenly found him in a snow hole still alive. Apparently during his climb he had got stuck half way up and decided to dig in until the weather improved. He was suffering badly from hypothermia and needed to be taken off the mountain as quickly as possible. We contacted the Sea King helicopter and luckily, in a small half hour window, they came in and took the climber to hospital for treatment. We were so pleased we had found him alive. "

The North Face Ridges of Ben Nevis

Jon climbing Castle Ridge Ben Nevis in winter

Jon under Carn Dearg Buttress, Ben Nevis with Tower Ridge in the background in winter.

One of the funniest rescues was on Glen Coe when a German climber had got stuck at the top of Central Gully at Buchailly Etive Mor. The RAF Team went up the Curved Ridge and the local Mountain Rescue Team went up the Central Buttress. As they got half way up, they realised the danger of starting an avalanche, so they were unable to continue the rescue. The leader of the local team decided they would dynamite the snow to prevent an avalanche.

He got the loud speaker out and shouted up to the German, "ACTUNG DON'T MOVE!!!"

They exploded the gully snow and then were able to ascend the ridge and buttress to rescue the German climber.

The Team's cover of the Highlands of Scotland had been quite eventful as they returned to RAF Leeming. They continued with their training and rescue missions, preparing for any circumstance they may come across in the field.

Jon explained about a special stretcher lowering practice off Mallon Cove, "It was a really scary experience when you were on the stretcher. You end up about 100 feet from the cliff face dangling in mid-air. I was always glad when it was over."

The rescues were not always on the hills and mountains, as one of these recoveries was a cave in the Derbyshire Dales. The accident involved a female who had been abseiling into the Lancaster pot hole but unfortunately she had forgotten to tie a knot in the bottom of the rope. She went straight off the end of it, falling about 90 feet plus but was still alive.

The team, together with the leader of the local Cave Rescue, went into the hole and stretchered her out of that deep cave and off to hospital for treatment. This was another experience for Jon in his role as a rescuer.

He returned on several occasions, during time off, to learn more about the cave systems in the Derbyshire Peak District. He enjoyed the adventure of discovering the complex world of the underground caves with their tunnels and water courses, diving through the many tunnels which were filled with water. His swimming prowess allowed him to go much deeper with the experts. The importance of going with a qualified person is paramount if you are going to stay safe.

Jon Ascending out of a Yorkshire Dales Pothole

Chapter 5: Bandits in Bolivia (First Accent Cerro Tiquimani South Face)

As I've said before Jon loved a challenge and when he got an invite to go on an expedition to Bolivia he jumped at the chance. The team consisted of eight RAF mountain rescue personnel. At 21 years of age Jon was the youngest of the team. It was planned to start on 30th May and would last seven weeks. It was winter in Bolivia but this had been chosen because it is the driest time of the year in the mountains. With all the sponsorship secured the team were now ready to go.

They flew out to La Paz, Bolivia, via Miami in the USA. La Paz airport is one of the highest in the world at 13,323 feet above sea level. La Paz, where the team were based, is 11,975 feet high and because of the rare atmosphere needs some time to acclimatise. When they got off the plane, everyone felt light headed as they carried their baggage across the tarmac. Two trucks arrived from the Club Andino Boliviano (CAB) who had been booked to help move all the equipment during the expedition. The President and a Team Leader, were there to help in transporting the teams around the vast mountain ranges during their time in Bolivia. Their wealth of knowledge of the terrain and weather was a great advantage to the team.

The first five days were spent adjusting to the lack of oxygen, finding the steep narrow streets of La Paz a real effort to walk around. During this time they sampled the local food and drink, observing the local culture. After two days they all started to wander around the slopes of La Paz, doing only short walks, completing their acclimatisation to the rare atmosphere.

On the fifth day the team felt ready to tackle the mountains. They set, off deciding to split into two groups and explore the mountains they had chosen to climb. Group 1, were driven to the Zonga Pass then into the Rio Zongo where they were dropped off on the path to Tiquimani. They ascended the path to Cerrol Ilampu near Tiquimani and camped near a stream.

Group 2, consisting of Jon, and three other members were dropped off near the north west slopes of Huayna Potosi. They then walked along an aqueduct towards the glacier which is just below Huayna Potosi. They camped near the glacier and one of the team inspected it before calling it a day. Another team member was now complaining of pain and was not well. The next morning, which was very cold, saw him much worse and he returned to La Paz accompanied by a friend, so he could receive some medical attention. That was the end of his expedition and he returned home to RAF Leeming the following evening so he could receive the proper treatment.

Jon and the other team member walked up the glacier checking out the lower slopes of Huayna Potosi. Another near miss on the glacier!! Jon was stood on what he thought was solid ice and snow but it was an ice bridge, which suddenly started cracking then gave way. Jon found himself falling down the crevasse but with presence of mind, he jammed his ice axes into both sides of the walls.

As he said to me on his return home, "I was lucky!! the crevasse wasn't very wide and I managed to get the ice axes into the sides which stopped my fall. I don't know how deep it was but I was able to climb out once I got my crampons into the iced sides. It was something you couldn't plan for. It didn't look anything like an ice bridge."

They returned to base camp optimistic of climbing Huayna Potosi the next day. They awoke next morning to thick cloud, high winds with sleet and snow falling. The sky didn't look good and as their colleague returned from La Paz, the remainder of the day was spent preparing for the rough weather that was closing in. That night, over twelve inches of snow fell on the camp. The next two days found them snowed in with no chance of climbing the mountain because of the danger of avalanches and poor visibility in the driving snow.

On the third day, they finally were able to break camp and make their way off the mountain. It took them nearly three hours to cover just two kilometres in the deep heavy snow. When they got to a place called Milluni, a passing truck gave them a lift back to La Paz.

The other group had the same problem with the weather and had to come off Cerro Japu Japuni mainly because they had equipment, clothes and two stoves stolen by local shepherds. They eventually got to Zongo Pass and awaited collection by CAB. The roads, by then, were just passable on their way back to La Paz.

The next two days were spent resting up and recovering waiting for the weather to clear. They reported the theft of the gear to the Police and then they relaxed, enjoying the city and its cosmopolitan atmosphere.

It was during this time that another life threatening experience happened to Jon. They had gone to a local night club and they bought their drinks on a tab which was kept behind the bar. At the end of the night they went to pay and the bill was over two hundred pounds. The guys stated they hadn't drunk that much beer and were not going to pay the full bill. They were suddenly surrounded, by what Jon described as bandits with machine guns, threatening to get the money one way or the other. After some quick negotiating with these gunmen, a team member was allowed to return to the hotel and get the money. Once they had paid the obvious extortionate price for their drinks they were released and needless to say didn't go back to the night club.

The next day, the team set off to climb Huayna Potosi by the normal route. They climbed up part of the mountain before returning to base camp, planning to reach the top on the following day. Jon and "Jiggsy" decided to ascend further up the mountain but had to retreat back down because of the heavy snow. It took them two days to climb and walk off the mountain with waist deep snow in places.

Jon climbing on Huayna Potosi

Jon climbing on Huayna Potosi

Jon was now feeling quite unwell with a nasty throat infection. The team returned to the Zongo Pass but Jon returned to La Paz in the vehicle to get some medical treatment. The next day they returned to the mountain and started preparing for the climb. The following two days saw them get to the top of Huayna Potosi and experience some stunning views of the Cordillera Real Range stretching northwards.

Returning to La Paz on the fourth day they found Jon was recovering well from his throat infection. They spent a further two days recovering from the climb and then got ready to climb Tiquimani.

The team split into two groups again with Jon and three colleagues attempting the unclimbed south face of Tiquimani. The other three team members intended climbing the normal route of Condoriri.

Jon's group camped at an idyllic spot, directly under Tiquimani's south face. The next morning, at 6 15am, saw Jon and Paul (Jiggsy) Jiggins set off to ascend the new route up the left side of the snow and glacier tongue which hangs down the south west face of the mountain. It was a tough climb but they reached the summit in good time, they then abseiled down the entire route which is a Scottish Grade 4 climb. They had achieved the first ascent of this difficult route on Tiquimani.

The next day the other two team members set off to make a first ascent of the south west ridge of Tiquimani. The weather was perfect and the bivouac site was on a large platform. The next morning at 8am saw the pair set off for the summit reaching it at 11 35am.

The following day sees them break camp and return to Rio Zongo ready to be picked up and transported back to La Paz. It was a successful four days on the mountain and all of them were ready for a well earned rest and recovery. They relaxed and enjoyed some good food, caught up on some much needed sleep and recollected on their achievements.

After two days in La Paz they took a minibus to a small fishing village called Copacabana, which was situated on the shores of Lake Titicaca. The team enjoyed the relaxing atmosphere at one of the highest freshwater lakes in the world with its panoramic views of this mountainous country. After three days of exploring the Kingdom of the Incas they returned to La Paz.

The day before they were due to fly home, the team went to a crag outcrop just outside La Paz and demonstrated mountain rescue and self rescue techniques to Club Andino Boliviano (CAB) members.

CAB were intending to set up a Mountain Rescue Section in Bolivia because there were none at that time.

The final evening, their Team Leader presented a slide show for the British Embassy staff and guests. At 5 30pm the following day they were all taken to the airport for the flight home.

This had been a successful expedition to Bolivia and Jon had gained a lot of mountain experience during the trip. He had escaped a fall down a crevasse and a fright with the bandit gunmen at a La Paz night club.

Tiquimani Jiggins/Ker Route (Scottish Grade 4)

Above picture shows the Route and First Ascent of the South West Face of Cerro Tiquimani

Above picture shows the Route and First Ascent of the South West Face of Cerro Tiquimani

Jon climbing the Scottish Grade 4, South West Face of Cerro Tiquimani

Jon climbing the South West Face of Cerro Tiquimani

Above and Below the sunset on Lake Titicaca, Bolivia

Lake Titticaca, Bolivia with Huayna Potosi in centre background

Chapter 6: Paramedic after RAF

On returning to Leeming, Jon was now looking to get promoted which would move him up to Deputy Team Leader. However he would need to become a Corporal before he could be promoted to Deputy Team Leader. Unfortunately he couldn't be promoted whilst in the Mountain Rescue Team which meant he would have to return to his basic role as a Motor Transport Driver.

The only vacancy at this time was at RAF Kinloss so Jon and his wife decided he would try and get his promotion there. They had lived at Burneston first before moving into a house on the RAF Leeming base. It was during their time at Burneston that Jon had bought another motorcycle, a Suzuki 600cc. There were some nasty bends on the way home from RAF Leeming and on a dark misty night Jon had another near miss when he failed to see the sharp bend and went straight through the fence and hedge. Again he was very lucky with just an injury to his right foot. The bike came off worse which led him to buy a flying machine in the form of a Suzuki GXR 750. It was a race track bike made road legal. I experienced the power when he gave me a go on it during a weekend visit home.

He was very reluctant to move but knew it was the only way to get promoted and try for a deputy team leader's spot on the Mountain Rescue Section. As a Corporal he would earn more money and hopefully get back into the job he loved.

He soon settled into his new job at RAF Kinloss, driving the huge tankers which were used to fuel up the massive transport aeroplanes. He would fill up these planes on a regular basis, gaining more experience within his trade. He also joined the Mountain Rescue

Section as a part time member. Team Leader Dave Whalley welcomed him on board because he knew of Jon's experiences.

It wasn't long though before he heard the bad news. All the driving jobs were going to be civilianised and there was no chance of him getting his promotion as his job would no longer exist. Also his wife was quite homesick because of the remoteness of Kinloss.

Jon then decided his days in the RAF were numbered so he applied for a discharge. It was granted and after a bad bout of glandular fever he left the RAF and moved to Alnwick.

It took him a few weeks to get over the glandular fever and now he was looking for work in Northumberland. He did several jobs around the area which included HGV driving, as he had all his Heavy Goods vehicle licences. He also worked as an assistant chef in a local restaurant, this skill had also been gained in the RAF when he had made breakfasts and other meals for the mountain rescue team when they were away from base.

This lasted for about a year but Jon wanted a permanent job and on a visit to the local job centre they offered him, that day, an interview with the Ambulance Service at Newcastle. The Manager of the Ambulance Service interviewed him and once he found out the job Jon had done in the RAF he knew this was a person he wanted on board. At the end of the interview he explained to Jon that he had been out with a mountain rescue team the previous weekend and knew how fit and capable rescuers they were.

He started his new job and moved house to Rothbury where he was stationed. He soon settled into his new role as an Ambulance Technician. Jon had always been a bright intelligent young boy sailing through exams at school without too much studying. He now set his sights on becoming a Paramedic in the Ambulance Service. He spent a lot of extra time at the Ambulance Station learning as much as possible about the job.

Jon also enjoyed the driving side of the job and because of his previous RAF experience he showed how capable he was behind the wheel. He had to complete an Advanced Driving Course with the Police and demonstrated his very good driving skills.

One of his early jobs he attended on the Ambulance was to a motorcycle crash. The young man had left the road and collided with the trees situated just off the carriageway. It was a real bad accident and he had no chance of surviving it.

This was the start of Jon attending quite a few fatal accidents and incidents. His work colleagues nicknamed him "Jinxy Jon" because of it. The next two years soon passed with lots of rescues dealing with heart attacks, road traffic accidents, farm and works incidents.

He attended numerous courses to improve his knowledge of clinical procedures and rescue techniques, which he was able to use at the scene of many incidents. Jon quickly learned all the new information and material he was given and it was now time for him to study for his paramedic examination.

One of the prerequisites was to conduct three anaesthetics on patients in hospital under the control and guidance of the anaesthetist in charge. As usual, Jon did more than he needed to, making him quite proficient at putting the patients to sleep, ready for their operation. He was also questioned in depth by Consultants regarding procedures and treatment of injured or sick patients. Each time he passed with flying colours, getting 100% for many of his examinations.

Successfully passing all his tests, Jon was now a qualified Paramedic and took charge at the scene of incidents when he was the only Paramedic on duty.

Another incident he attended, related to a hang glider pilot who had ended up lodged in some very high trees. When he got there the Fire Brigade were trying to work out how to get the pilot down. The extendable ladder on the large truck couldn't get near enough to make a rescue because of the trees. They also didn't know the extent of the pilot's injuries either. Jon's previous experiences and training in the RAF Mountain Rescue gave the Fire Brigade an option to complete the task.

Jon, with two climbing ropes around his body, started to scale up the trees towards the stranded hang glider pilot. He quickly assessed the pilot and found he wasn't too badly injured, more shocked and shaken than anything else. Jon explained to him what he was about to do to get him safely to the ground. He then set about fixing the first rope across and above the glider and using the other rope, he abseiled down to the pilot, removed him from the hang glider then took him to the safety of the ground below.

The Fire Brigade Officers were well impressed with the rescue and asked Jon to show them how he had achieved it. It was a rescue he had trained and accomplished in the Mountains of the Lake District and Scotland many times during his period in the RAF Mountain Rescue Section.

Chapter 7: Paramedic on Air Ambulance

Jon was always looking for a new challenge in the rescue service. He had always been interested in flying, probably stemmed from the time when we went to Malta on holiday and during the flight he was allowed to spend some time in the cockpit of the large passenger aeroplane. A thrilling experience for a twelve year old. He had also joined the RAF because of the flying involved.

There was one Air Ambulance in the North East, which was based at Blyth in Northumberland, so Jon volunteered to work on the Air Ambulance during his days off. His skills of reading maps gained during his RAF Mountain Rescue days and his Paramedic abilities made him an ideal person for the work. He was also very capable of multi-tasking during flight and thoroughly enjoyed the new experience.

Jon was enjoying the flying so much he decided to learn how to fly a microlight. He had a specialist parachute which he used for parascending off the hillsides near Simonside in Northumberland. The only problem with it was you could only fly when the wind and air currents were right. So flying a microlight was the next step, giving him more freedom in the air. He soon had the take-off and landing mastered with his newly purchased flexi-wing microlight. Initially he flew in and around Eshott airfield which is situated just off the A1 near Felton, Northumberland. His friends soon had him flying further afield to Carlisle Airport.

I remember going on my first flight with him, which was really exhilarating. I got some great aerial photographs as we flew up the beautiful Northumberland coast, from Warkworth to Holy Island then headed inland to Alnwick Castle. A second flight on another day took us over to Rothbury and the Simonside Hills where we experienced quite a bit of turbulence. He was very skilled at flying the microlight, with the take-off and landing so smooth. Jon also took his mother up for a flight around Eshott. She was impressed and enjoyed her flight.

The next thing Jon planned was a flight to Spain with his friends. They flew down to Lincoln to pick up another pilot, then headed for the English Channel intending to cross over to Dunkirk. As they got near to London Jon lost sight of the other microlights.

Jon explained, "I lost sight of them as we tried to fly around Heathrow. The next thing I knew, there was a great big Jumbo jet about five hundred feet above me. It looked massive as it passed over me. I eventually got back on the right route and joined the others."

Another near miss!!

They stopped at a small airfield in Kent before crossing the English Channel. It was at this time that Eddie and John Hood noticed Jon didn't have a lifejacket for the crossing. So they wound him up by saying he must have something attached to him to keep him afloat if he ditched in the Channel. They got him to tie several large plastic containers around his waist just before they set off. He took it in hook, line and sinker giving everyone a good laugh as they landed on French soil.

They flew on through France and into Spain. Jon had now purchased a lifejacket for the return trip. It took them about a week of travelling before they made their way back onto home soil across the English Channel. As they started to negotiate the crossing they ran into some really poor weather conditions. Jon again lost sight of the others and ended up landing next to a small static caravan site. The owner was very friendly and interested in his trip. He also allowed Jon to stay in one of the empty caravans overnight. The next morning he provided Jon with a full English breakfast. The other microlights had landed on the planned airfield.

As Jon said, "They were very jealous of me, when they heard what I had had for breakfast and they had only been given some toast."

The flight home was uneventful as they landed at Eshott safely. Jon had really enjoyed the freedom of flying over Europe which led him to continue exploring England and into Scotland improving his ability in the skies. He also planned, with his friends, another trip which would take them into Italy.

Over the next five years Jon continued to work at Rothbury and worked more and more shifts on the Air Ambulance.

One morning whilst in the Blyth Air Support Unit Office, Jon had noticed the bad weather which was gathering some ten miles west of them. They had had some sunshine at Blyth but it was a totally different story that short distance to the west. Ambulance control had telephoned Jon about ten o'clock and advised him to make tracks for home as it was snowing heavily around Rothbury. He decided to contact the Police Air Support Unit before setting off for home because they would have the latest on the weather conditions in the region. When he told them he was heading for Rothbury they just laughed, stating he had no chance of getting there as all the roads in and out Rothbury were blocked with snow. Jon thought that's me not been able to get home tonight.

The Engineer and Pilot had been working on the helicopter all morning and were just finishing off the blade tracking when the emergency telephone rang. It was now about 2 40pm in the afternoon and the request was for the Air Ambulance to attend an isolated farm in the wilds of Northumberland, where a young woman was in labour with her first child. Jon, the Pilot and the other Paramedic had no idea where this farm was located but control were going to give them a grid reference.

They accepted the job and started the aircraft up ready for takeoff. As they received the grid reference, they were informed that the road ambulance had got stuck in a snow drift on the way to the farm and the local Police four wheel drive vehicle had also been abandoned. They were in liaison with the local Search and Rescue Team who were going to try and make it on foot to the farm.

The helicopter took off as Jon studied the Ordinance Survey maps and found the farm in the Cheviot Hills. The Pilot entered the location into the GPS informing his crew they would be there in seventeen minutes but, as they flew west, the weather was right down to the ground so they couldn't fly direct to the farm. Jon had to work out the route they would have to take, which saw them following the A1 north to Alnwick. They then turned west following the line of the low tension wires which run across the countryside. Hopefully by doing this they could skirt around the high ground where visibility was now down to zero.

Jon contacted Ambulance Control informing them of the weather conditions and that they couldn't give an ETA (Estimated Time of Arrival) or even a guarantee they could even get there. As they flew on, Jon realised they were flying straight into a snow storm. He kept ticking off the landmarks while the Pilot and the other Paramedic kept their eyes glued on the wires and pylons they were now flying below due to poor visibility.

The Helicopter was now flying at a reduced speed and height as they tried to keep the wires and pylons in sight. Jon confirmed with the Pilot that he needed to keep flying west until they reached and hopefully found the A697.

Finding the A697 was so important because if they missed it, the Cheviot Hills were only a couple of miles west and they would be flying blind straight into them. Because so much snow had fallen and the fact there was no traffic moving on these roads it was a nightmare picking out the actual road to follow. Suddenly they spotted a road and the Pilot circled two or three times to check if it was the road they needed to follow. The discussion between the three men was quite tense as it was stressful flying in the atrocious conditions.

It appeared to be the A697 so they turned north heading for Wooler. A frantic shout "WIRES" caused the Pilot to slam the anchors on, bringing the helicopter back to a hover. It was now decision time. They couldn't fly over the pylons and wires because of the low heavy cloud, which were filled with snow, so to carry on, they would have to fly under them.

The thought of a young women in labour with her first child made up their minds. The Pilot hover taxied twenty feet from the ground under the wires, then climbed up to a hundred feet flying north past Wooler.

Jon informed the team to look out for the first road left which would have a small river running parallel to it. By now they were heading towards the hills again and the cloud base was much lower. When they spotted the river the helicopter was down to about forty to fifty feet from the ground. There was no sign of the road so they followed the river west as Jon scrutinised the maps for any hazards ahead.

The Pilot piped up, "We've just passed a fork in the river and the river valley is getting tighter and steeper. I am not happy in here, it can't be right Jon."

After checking the maps again Jon confirmed they needed to go back to the fork in the river and fly west instead of the southerly direction they had taken. Returning to the fork in the river they took the other route. They soon found themselves approaching the farm and reflected they had made the right decision to carry on, as this was no place to have your first child at the best of times let alone in these conditions. The farm was in the middle of nowhere and only the helicopter could have got through in the snowbound conditions.

They landed in the field next to the farm cottages and the Paramedics jumped out, landing almost waist deep in the freshly laid snow. They soon had their patient onboard the helicopter and just in time as the contractions were every five minutes. The husband told them that all the electricity and telephone lines were down and his mobile phone had run out during his call to the Ambulance.

The seventeen minutes to the farm had taken one hour and five minutes, everyone hoped it would not take that long on the way back to the hospital, especially with the condition of the pregnant patient. A mid-flight birth would be a real challenge. They took off, leaving the poor farmer with no way of communicating with his wife or the hospital.

They headed back along the river valley and as they approached the A697 the visibility was starting to improve all the time. This allowed Jon to plot a direct course to the Hospital. After ten minutes in the sky they ran into clear weather and Jon contacted Ambulance Control, asking for a road vehicle to meet them at the helipad. It had taken only twenty minutes and the farmer's wife was safely in the hospital much to the relief of the helicopter crew. Later that afternoon she had a healthy baby boy.

The crew were later presented with an Emergency Services Award for this call out.

A lot was learned that day about working as a team, trusting implicitly in your colleagues and how you need, sometimes, to stick your neck out a little bit, to get a difficult job done.

About this time the Great North Air Ambulance Charity was looking to employ full time Paramedics to staff their helicopter based at Teesside Airport. Jon applied and was offered one of the jobs.

Jon soon found himself treating injured motorcyclists on the North Yorkshire Moor roads, which claim several lives each year. These roads are so remote, the Air Ambulance is the quickest transport to Specialist Hospitals like James Cook, Middlesbrough, with its Helipad right outside the Accident and Emergency Department. It was during this time that Jon's friend Jim Martin started working on the Air Ambulance. Jim had worked on the Police Helicopter before joining the Great North Air Ambulance.

On the Great North Air Ambulance trained volunteer Trauma Doctors were now on board, as other Air Ambulances across the country. Jon also did a four week exchange to the HEMS (Helicopter Emergency Medical Service) in London. This enabled him to gain valuable experience with the Trauma Doctors who work in the London area. The dedicated Doctors had lots of expertise in dealing with all sorts of trauma and

Jon pumped them with questions to gather as much information in the treatment of major trauma.

This knowledge was to prove invaluable as not long after returning from London, the Great North Air Ambulance was called to a head on car crash on the North Yorkshire Moors. A Doctor and Jon were the medics. When they arrived they found a woman in her thirties trapped in her car with head injuries. As they treated her Jon noticed how agitated she was and realised she had a serious head injury.

The Fire Brigade soon had her freed from the car and the Doctor with Jon started to anaesthetise her, to hopefully slow the bleeding in her brain. Jon found a vein in her arm and the Doctor put her to sleep with an adequate dose of anaesthetic. Jon was now manually keeping her breathing and they started to load the stretcher onto the helicopter.

Once everyone was in place, the Great North Air Ambulance took off and headed straight to James Cook University Hospital, where a Specialist Consultant was waiting ready to treat the injured woman. Jon and the Doctor kept a close eye on their patient as the treatment continued on route to the Hospital.

The Helipad at James Cook is directly outside the Accident and Emergency Department, so as soon as they landed, it was a quick transfer from the helicopter to Accident and Emergency. On leaving, they didn't know whether she would survive but left her in the safe hands of the Consultant. They climbed back into the helicopter, stopping all the traffic again as they took off from the Middlesbrough Hospital heading back to Teesside Airport where the aircraft was housed.

The next day Jon and the Air Ambulance were requested to take a man with a suspected heart attack to James Cook Hospital and again they landed outside the

Accident and Emergency Department. Whilst there, Jon made some enquires about the woman he had brought in the previous day. He then visited her on the ward where she was recovering. She was sitting up quite chirpy in her hospital bed, was delighted to see him and thanked him for saving her life. She had suffered some brain trauma but putting her to sleep had aided her rapid recovery. Jon left the hospital feeling very satisfied, the treatment they had given to her had been appropriate and adequate, she would be leaving hospital soon, fully recovered.

He was again working with Jim on the Great North Air Ambulance and would question him regularly about the flying of the helicopter. He had mastered flying his microlight and plans to fly further afield with it were well advanced.

Chapter 8: Flight to Italy in Microlight

The planned microlight trip to Italy was now here and Jon together with Eddie McCallam and John Hood did the final preparations at Eddie's airfield strip near Long Framlington. They had arranged to meet their friends in Lincolnshire on their way, before crossing the English Channel.

A new adventure started as Jon, Eddie and John set off flying due south, which would keep them away from any major airports. They first landed at Bagby airstrip in North Yorkshire, taking about an hour and a half break, before heading for Headon in Nottinghamshire then onto Stapleford in Lincolnshire. After meeting their friends they took off for Abbeville in France. They crossed the English Channel without incident landing at Abberville about nine o'clock at night.

Having stayed overnight on the outskirts of Abbeville they flew off southwards down the Rhone Valley to Nangis, which took them a couple of hours. Late afternoon saw them flying south east to Pouilly Maconge and after a short stop they flew onto Chalon-Sur-Saone. It was now seven o'clock in the evening so they stayed overnight sampling the local food and drink.

The next day saw them heading due south for Montelimar and the Mediterranean Sea. After a couple of hours break they set off, landing two hours later at a small glider club near to Fayence.

Once refuelled they flew off in the direction of Monaco where the F1 Grand Prix was being held. Knowing they couldn't fly over Monaco, the group made their way out to sea flying along the coast towards Pisa in Italy. They then flew inland to Tuscany flying over the famous San Marino Grand Prix Circuit.

The next couple of days saw them head east towards the coast of Rimini and due to the build up of wind all microlights landed at the small airfield of Fano. One of the pilots had bent his wing on landing, he just straightened it himself making the plane ready and safe for flying. At this point in time, the whole group were given a warning about being in Italian Air Space, as they all set off again heading for Venice.

They decided to leave Italy and headed for Portoroz in Slovinia staying there overnight. The weather was changing for the worse, so the next day they headed for a small Airport at Celje. They had just landed when the storm made its way into the area. There was a children's party going on in the large hangar but the families interrupted it to let Jon and his friends put their microlights under shelter as the storm came thundering in.

As Jon said, "If we hadn't got the planes into the hangar straight away, they would have been smashed to bits by the violent storm. We just got to Celje in time as it followed us in."

The next day the weather had cleared and the group decided to make their way back home. They set off and flew through Austria, then into Germany. The fine weather started to deteriorate as they approached Frankfurt, so finding a small airfield nearby they set down waiting for the storm to pass.

As the sky cleared the team took off and headed towards Belgium. Just after passing over a large power station one of the team's engines cut out and he had to land in a field. He hadn't actually run out of fuel but had forgotten to prime both tanks of the two stroke engine, so when the first tank ran out the fuel stopped coming through, thereby stalling the plane.

Jon stated, "It was a good job it didn't run out over the Power Station or he would have ended up inside one of the giant towers."

They were soon off again but due to the rough bumps from the mountains they were flying through, a decision was made to head towards Aachen. As they got near to Aachen two Military helicopters appeared alongside the group of microlights and ordered them all to land at the local airport. A full check of their flight plans was taken and after having knuckles rapped for not informing the authorities and getting permission to fly over Germany, they were sent on their way out of Germany into Belgium.

It was now a short trip across Belgium to Calais and across the English Channel landing at Headcorn in Kent. After a short break they flew due north west to Sibson staying there for the night. An early start from Sibson saw the group heading north with Jon's friends dropping off home in Lincoln. Jon, Eddie and John continued to Bagby, resting there for a short while before flying home to the Longframlington Airstrip. It had been a good trip, seeing all the sights, in the Rhone Valley, Monaco, San Marino, Slovinia, Germany and Belgium.

Chapter 9: Flight to North Cape of Norway (First Person to fly there by Microlight)

Next was the big challenge to fly by flexi-wing microlight to the "North Cape, 70 degrees North" as on the television programme. Jon believed it would be a first, as he hadn't heard of anyone doing it before. It all came about after a night in the pub, when the extraordinary journey was put together. He had to find some others who were as crazy as him to partake in the adventure. Eddie McCallam was first on the list, then two other friends were persuaded to join in.

The plan of action was to fly north to Shetland, fill up with fuel, then set off across the North Sea to Bergen. Refuel, then follow the West Coast of Norway right up to the North Cape. They would then fly into Finland, Sweden, Estonia, Latvia, Lithuania, Russia, Poland, Denmark, Germany, Netherlands and back across the North Sea into East Anglia.

The main worry about the trip was crossing the North Sea both ways. The wind direction would play a big part in their flight across this vast expanse of water.

Jon commented, "If the wind is against us, we won't have enough fuel to get across the North Sea, as I think we'll just have enough to make it to Bergen with a following wind."

They decided it had to be June when the journey would hopefully have warmer weather, as the sun never sets at the North Cape.

It was late June 2002, everything was packed and ready for the massive undertaking of flying to the North Cape. Jon, Eddie, and their two friends had done their final checks on the flexi-wings, so it was time to set off heading north for Shetland. They landed mid-afternoon on Shetland and filled up the tanks of the microlights. They stayed there overnight and flew out early next morning heading across the North Sea to Bergen. The weather was quite good as they started their trip and the wind was blowing westerly so the fuel would not be a problem.

As they got near to Norway the wind had dropped and suddenly they flew into thick fog. They all dropped height where the visibility was better but as Jon said, "We could only see about 100 yards in front of us as we headed east towards Bergen."

By late evening they had arrived safely in Bergen as the mist had lifted when they reached land. What they didn't know was how close they were to the Oil Rigs in the North Sea, if they had hit one of those in the mist it would have been curtains for them all. Housing the planes in a small hangar they got a taxi and went into the town centre to get some food and find a bed for the night.

Next morning saw them up early and with a good breakfast inside them they took off and headed for the airfield at Bodo. Following the west coast of Norway they travelled most of the day reaching Bodo airport late afternoon. One thing was apparent, the climate was much colder as they moved northward towards the Pole. They were now in the Artic Circle.

Again it had been a long day, so a decision was made that the next day would be much shorter and it was agreed to travel near Narvik to a small airfield called Framnes. The four of them waited for the day to warm up before setting off, aware it was a much shorter flight to Framnes.

As they took off, little did Jon and Eddie know another near miss was about to happen. First I must tell you a little about the regalia the pilots were wearing. They had been given Emerson survival suits for the trip, just in case they had to ditch into the sea or Fjord. These suits, which are bright yellow in colour, increase the survival time in the icy water, they have seals at the wrist, neck and hood. However, they are very cumbersome and were nick-named by the group "Blobby" suits. There were the usual pockets on the outside, with one of the side pockets containing an eight foot lanyard which is securely attached to the suit.

Eddie was now flying Jon's microlight, giving him a rest and allowing him to view and enjoy the spectacular scenery. The flight was smooth as they followed the coastline north but it was soon to change. Unaware to both Jon and Eddie, Jon's lanyard was slowly working its way out of his pocket heading over the engine towards the propeller. All of a sudden there was an almighty bang, Jon was pulled half out of his seat, backwards towards the engine and propeller. Only his seat belt saved him from being dragged out of the aeroplane into the propeller and certain death.

They still had no idea what had happened as the plane was flying as normal, so they carried on with their intended journey.

John was telling Eddie, "It was like my suit had a mind of its own and wanted to leave the plane."

Eddie thought, "I'm not superstitious, but I did tell him to tighten his harness belt up, before we took off."

Staying away from the mountains, which causes a lot of turbulence to the small microlights, their aviation took them along Ofotfjord to their destination airfield, which was situated on a peninsular west of Norvik.

On landing both pilots walked round to the rear of the aeroplane and found the culprit of the incident. The eight foot lanyard was wrapped round the boss of the propeller but fortunately no damage was caused to any part of the engine or propeller shaft. They just looked at each other in amazement, cracking up in hysterical laughter, thinking to themselves how lucky they had been.

The next day saw them in the air heading towards Tromso, which has one of the bigger airports in Norway. Heading west first along the Ofotfjord, then north once they had reached the coast. Their flight path took them up the rugged coastline, which looks out across the Norwegian Sea, to the small island of Hekkingen where they turned east and followed the fjords to Tromso. Arriving mid-afternoon gave them time to park the microlights, view the local sights and find accommodation for that night.

Their plan for the following day was to travel north east to Hammerfest, which was the final stop before reaching the North Cape. The journey saw them track the waterways, which are part of the Norwegian Sea, leading the team to Hammerfest airfield without having to go out into the open sea.

Landing in good time at Hammerfest, over a substantial Norwegian meal, they charted the final leg to 70 degrees North.

Valan, Hannigsvag airstrip is the nearest one to the North Cape, so the group decided they would fly to 70 degrees North first, then south to Valan airfield and spend the night in Hannigsvag.

The next morning saw them flying north east towards the North Cape.

Jon remarked, "It's the coldest air I've ever experienced, even though the sun was shining. The cliffs are dramatic as they come straight out of the sea, I got some photos as we went past them. We then flew down to Vanal Airport at Hannigsvag and it was still freezing there."

He went on to say, "Even on the top of Tiquimani in Bolivia it wasn't as cold as it was at the North Cape."

They all went down to a local public house in Hannigsvag and had a meal.

Jon commented, "We stayed there most of the night. It was full of young local men and our meal was whale meat. It tasted just like liver and wasn't too bad to eat. It certainly filled us up. The pub stayed open all night with the locals drinking all the way through. We headed back to the airfield late on and rested up for the next leg of the trip to Pajala in Sweden."

Lunchtime the next day saw the microlights setting off heading for Pajala. They were away from the mountains now so the journey was fairly smooth as they soared southwards towards their destination. It was a small airstrip at Pajala and after landing they found a small hotel nestled in the nearby forest. After a good night's sleep, which they needed, their plan was to fly south to Vaasa in Finland.

The route, as the crow flies, took them over the northern part of the Baltic Sea and into Finland. The town of Vaasa juts out into the Gulf of Bothnia, which is part of the Baltic Sea. The airport is four miles south and they all landed safely parking up for the night. A local taxi took them to Vaasa town centre and they found a local hotel to stay at overnight. Once they had washed and cleaned up they found a local night club in which to relax. They had a really good night chatting away about the journey so far and where their next destination would be.

Fairly early the next morning saw them ready to set off for Turku, which is still in Finland but they were hoping to make their way to Tallinn in Estonia by teatime.

By lunchtime the team had reached Turku airport. They landed and started to file a flight plan with Tallinn Airport before flying into Estonia. Having filed all the details with the Authorities, it was just a matter of waiting for permission to enter the country.

One of the team said, "I've just found the cloakroom ticket for my fleece. I've left it in the night club at Vaasa and it's got my passport in it."

A long discussion took place as to whether they would fly back for the passport or risk entry into Estonia without it. They decided to risk it hoping the Authorities wouldn't check up. It was about an hour when the go ahead was given for them to fly to Tallinn. It didn't take them long because they flew directly over the Baltic Sea missing out Helsinki. Unfortunately for them, on landing at Lennart Menri Airport at Tallinn, the Authorities conducted a routine check and found one member of the team did not have a passport. They were all arrested and held in a detention room. It was explained to the Officers what had happened and they were allowed to ring the Hotel in Vaasa and ask them to contact the night club and retrieve his passport.

The hotel called back stating they had got the passport and had managed to get it onto a flight which was on its way to Helsinki. The team member was then allowed to fly into Helsinki Airport and collect his passport from the Authorities. He was given quite a grilling from the Finnish Border Control Officer because he had left Finland without a passport. Eventually he was allowed to return to his colleagues at Tallinn.

Everyone was relieved the matter was now sorted out. They set off the next morning for Parnu, which is situated towards the southern end of Estonia. After an overnight stop they flew down the coastline of the Gulf of Riga, which is part of the Baltic Sea, landing at Riga Airport where they refuelled all the planes. The next morning saw them in the air by noon flying down to Kaunas airfield in Lithuania.

From Kaunas they flew to Kaliningrad which is part of Russia, landing late afternoon. The plan for the next day was to fly to Grudziadz, Poland. However they changed their minds and landed at a small glider airfield on route. The gliders were flying and Jon went up in the towing aeroplane to experience what it was like pulling the glider up into the sky.

The following day saw them airborne again heading towards Grudziadz and for the first time the weather was not that good.

Next morning they set off for Pila, still in Poland and managed to get there before the weather closed in on them. The bad weather lasted for over two days, so they just had to sit it out and wait for the skies to clear.

After three days they took off for Goleniow Airport, Szczecin. Landing only to refuel, they were soon back in the air heading for Neubrandenburg in Germany. Staying there overnight the guys decided to fly into Denmark the next day. They would fly north west, cross the Baltic Sea and land at the Lolland Falster Airport near Gammel Holeby in Denmark. This would be another country in the log book. Mid-morning the next day saw them set off for Lolland Falster landing safely about two hours later. Unfortunately they hadn't put in the correct flight plans to Lolland Falster and were promptly told to leave Denmark and return to Germany by the Authorities at the Airport.

In less than an hour they were back in the air sending their flight plans as they travelled. They headed towards Bremerhaven Airport in Germany but were going to land on a grassed airfield across the River Weser mouth which leads to the North Sea. The team landed at Segelfluggelande Blexen Flugglatz airfield and parked their microlights up in a safe place. They proceeded into the local town of Blexen and got themselves some food and then went to the local hostelry for a quiet drink.

The next day saw them heading for another grassed airfield at Texel in the Netherlands, which was situated on a small outcrop island in the north west of the country. They filled up there to make sure they had enough fuel for the journey home.

The next flight was across the North Sea but the team had to wait because of the strong headwind and poor visibility. It was now like the start of their epic journey, crossing the North Sea hung in the balance because their fuel would run out before they reached Norwich Airport if they tried it against a strong wind. After about three hours the weather changed, the wind dropped and the visibility improved, so the group of microlights flew into the sky and off across the sea.

Landing at Norwich Airport, they gave out a great sigh of relief, having managed the penultimate part of the journey without incident. They refuelled the planes and set off north.

Jon and Eddie headed for Teesside Airport, where as a family we were there to meet them. Also Jon's Boss was there and had kindly arranged for us to be on the tarmac when they landed. We were first told they were approaching the airfield and then saw the tiny dot of the microlight as it flew to the part of the Airport where the Great North Air Ambulance Helicopter was housed. It was a relief to see Jon safely home, after an astronomic journey which saw him visiting eleven

European countries. After a short rest and refuel, we waved him off as he and Eddie flew back home to Northumberland.

Chapter 10: Death of friend climbing Ben Nevis (National Bravery Award)

It was now back to work for Jon after his adventure. He was now based at Penrith and soon back out there dealing with all types of trauma, which was part of his every day job.

One interesting rescue involved the skill of Jim as a helicopter pilot, when Jon and him were sent to the mountain Helvellyn in the Lake District. Apparently a walker had been traversing Striding Edge on Helvellyn, when he fell and damaged his ankle. It was so bad he could not put any weight on it at all, which meant he would have to be carried off the mountain.

The mountain Helvellyn is 3118 feet/950 metres above sea level. Striding Edge is a narrow path, leading north west towards Thirlmere Lake, which drops away steeply on both sides, leaving it exposed to the elements even on the calmest of days. Many hikers have been blown off the ridge during stormy weather and some have died as a result of their fall. Jon and Jim had a discussion as they hovered above the injured person on how they were going to accomplish the rescue.

Jim said, "I can land it on the path as narrow as it is, but I'll have to keep the engine going to make sure I'm not blown off. If you can get the person on board as quickly as possible we will make it."

Jon replied, "That's fine by me, let's do it."

Jim landed the Great North Air Ambulance precariously on the mountain path. Jon jumped out of the helicopter and like a mountain goat he soon reached the injured walker. He quickly treated his patient and got him back to the helicopter as quickly as he could. Jim had held the copter steady and once the injured patient was on board safely strapped in, they took off for the Westmorland Hospital where he received the necessary treatment in the Accident and Emergency Department. It had been a difficult rescue but produced the desired result getting the patient off the mountain very quickly.

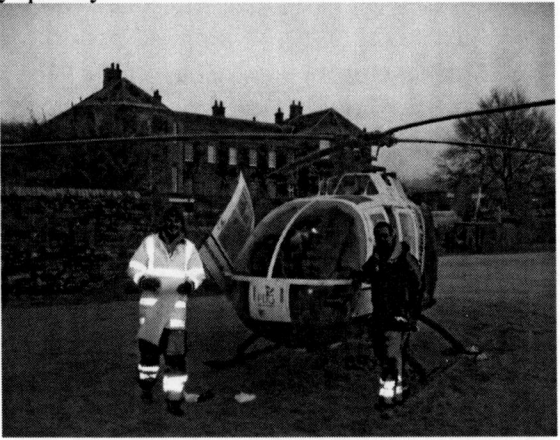

Jon and Jim at Cumbria Police Headquarters Penrith with the Great North Air Ambulance.

Jon and the Great North Air Ambulance making a rescue at Sty Head in the Lake District

There was a good team at Penrith, with a Doctor friend joining Jon on the medical side when he could get away from his day job. Also Jim had a very good helicopter pilot working on the Great North Air Ambulance when he was taking his days off. They all became good friends, which led to Jon's next project - learning to fly a helicopter.

Jon was quite happy at Penrith mixing and chatting to the Senior Police Officers who worked at the Police Headquarters. He continued to climb in the Lake District, which was right on his doorstep, during his days off. This led to his next near miss which ended in tragedy. It involved Jon, Jim and his Doctor pal.

The friends decided to attempt to climb Tower Ridge on Ben Nevis in January, which is a real hard winter climb. It has sufficient length and exposure to be classed as Alpine in the winter months, with its 2,000 foot pitch wall which faces North.

They started training for the winter ascent of Tower Ridge, attending the climbing wall at Penrith three times a week. This built up the muscle strength, stamina and agility they would need for the climb.

January soon came round and they were ready for their task. It was late January when they drove up to Fort William in Scotland to tackle "The Ben."

The group were Jon, Jim, his pal and wife and another friend. They booked into the hotel and settled down for the evening. The weather forecast wasn't good for the following day but the men decided to try the climb anyway. Apparently Ben Nevis was covered in ice and snow so they would need ice axes and crampons.

At ten o'clock the next morning saw them ready with all their kit for the difficult ascent ahead. The two ladies dropped the guys off at the Torlundy car park, which is on the north side of Ben Nevis. From the car park you have fairly easy access to Tower Ridge, so off the climbers went, intending to walk back to Fort William after they had scaled the buttress.

They were soon at the Tower Gully with the Douglas Boulder directly ahead. As they prepared for the climb, Jon's pal informed him and Jim he had forgotten to put his helmet in his bag. A discussion took place and he decided to carry on with the task ahead. Making their way across the gully, they started the ascent of the Douglas Boulder, which is part of the Tower Ridge. Jon realised straight away that the conditions were far from perfect so a lot of caution was taken as they made their way up the mountain.

The weather was turning for the worse, with the cloud starting to move down towards them from the summit. They hadn't reached halfway when Jon made the decision to abandon the climb, because the ice and freezing cloud was making it impossible to go any higher on the ridge. They moved back to the Douglas

Gap and Jon suggested abseiling into the Douglas Gully where it would be safer to descend off the dangerous terrain.

The nod of approval was quickly given and the friends decided there and then they would come back in February when the weather was hopefully kinder and climb it again. Jon put the rope around the rock they were standing on. Also on this arête was a sling, which had been there ever since Jon had been climbing Ben Nevis.

In Jon's words, "That sling has been fixed to the rock for years. Everyone uses it because it gives some protection when crossing the Douglas Gap. It must have been there for thirty years."

Jon clipped his rope into the sling and slowly lowered himself over the edge of the arête. He started cautiously down the gully, making sure he had good holds as he descended. After about twenty or thirty feet of his descent, he felt a sudden movement of the rock above then his rope went slack. Jon knew straight away what was happening because the same thing had happened on the Aiguille du Midi in the Alps when he was seriously injured. He reacted immediately, letting go of the rope he grabbed hold of the cliff, wedging his fingers and feet into the crevices of the rock face.

Jon describes what was happening and his feelings, "As I clung to the rock face, I first saw the block go past me, then my pal was falling after it. I could see his face clearly, as he looked at me, he seemed to say I'm going to die. Then, as he vanished down the gully, I felt a hard impact on my back and pain in my left hand, as Jim clattered into me as he fell. I managed to hang onto the rock and Jim was gone. I waited to be dragged off, because my rope was still attached to me, but as the rope whipped through and out of the karabiner, I realised the sling must have been cut by the block. I could hear it crashing its way down the mountain, then everything went quiet. "

His mind started racing, were both his friends dead, his pal had the only mobile, should he jump down and ring for help. The mobile might be broken; he would certainly break his legs jumping off and down the gully. He couldn't hang on much longer where he was, so he looked for a ledge which would allow him to sit and rest.

The arête had left quite a deep cavity, so Jon started to gingerly climb up towards it. His left hand was hurting a lot as he climbed and he noticed blood coming through the glove he was wearing. He managed to reach the ledge and pull himself up over the lip, sitting down on it with his legs dangling over the edge. He first checked his hand which was throbbing from the climb. When he took the glove off, he could see his bones and tendons of his thumb and forefinger. The skin had been ripped back, probably from Jim's crampons, Jon pulled it back over the gap and put his glove back on. His thoughts went back to his friends who he presumed to be dead. He started to prepare himself for a long cold wait for the Mountain Rescue Team. He estimated they would get to him about midnight but he had a bivi survival bag, food and water so it wasn't a problem. He had camped like this many times below Tower Ridge.

Looking down Tower Ridge from the Top of Ben Nevis

He settled down to wait when suddenly from the gully below he heard a shout.

"Jon, Jon are you there." It was Jim, he was still alive.

Jon replied, "Jim, How are you? How badly are you hurt?"

Jim replied, "I can move one arm and just about one leg but I'm in a bad way. There is something wrong with my hips."

Jon was amazed Jim was still alive but knew, from years of training and climbing in the mountains, that Jim wouldn't survive until midnight. His knowledge of Ben Nevis was now crucial, so he could make an attempt to get Jim rescued before he was killed by hypothermia. The other problem Jon had on his mind was the injury to Jim's hips, which could mean he had broken his pelvis and there was a possibility of blood loss from the many blood vessels in that area of the body.

Without ropes Jon knew he couldn't climb down from his present position, however if he climbed back up towards Douglas Gap, there was a traverse route he perhaps could clamber across, which leads to Observatory Gully. Once in the gully he would be able to slide down the snow and ice using his ice axes. Then he could reach the Charles Inglis Clark Memorial (CIC) hut and call for help.

Jon called back to Jim, "I'm going to try and get help by climbing out of here."

Jon started his climb, which was about one hundred and fifty to two hundred feet, to the point where he found the traverse. His left hand was agony and it had started bleeding again but that didn't matter, he needed to get off the mountain and call for help. The traverse was harder than he expected because he had to use his right hand only to strike the ice axe into the frozen snow and ice. (Jon is left handed)

As he moved out onto the traverse route he thought "I'm committed now just go for it."

It took Jon longer than normal to complete the traverse because he had no protection and one slip would mean no rescue for Jim and possible death for himself. Each time he stuck the ice axe in, he checked it a couple of times to make sure it would hold, moving sideways on across the ice and rock towards Observatory Gully. He had a couple of scares along the way when his feet slipped on the treacherous icy mountainside. After almost an hour and half, he reached the gully and was glad to jump down onto his feet. Jon quickly descended down the snow and ice. As he reached the bottom of Observatory Gully he knew Jim was not far away but when he shouted his name there was no reply.

His thoughts were, "I've got to get to the CIC hut as soon as possible."

He quickened his pace on the slope and reached the CIC hut in one piece. Going straight into the hut, he found the radio and following the instructions, he called the Police at Fort William, outlining what had happened on Tower Ridge. He waited for a reply but none came, so he called again asking urgently for help. The radio stayed silent. It was at this point that he started to go into shock from the ordeal.

He explained, "All of a sudden my legs started to shake, I felt sick and light headed, I knew I was going into shock so I had to do something. I remembered seeing some climbers making their way off the Ben as we started up the Douglas Boulder. I knew they would still be on the lower slopes of the Ben, so I set off running down the mountain to catch them up, which took my mind off the onset of shock."

Jon made good time as he followed the stream towards the Torlundy forest and car park. As he approached the forest he saw the climbers. He shouted over to them but they didn't hear him for the rushing stream. He sprinted after them catching up before they entered the trees.

He pleaded to them for the use of a phone stating, "I need to make an emergency call, I'll tell you about it in a minute."

One of the group gave him a mobile and Jon rang the Police, explaining to the operator what had happened on the mountain. As he was speaking to the Police control, he heard, then saw the Sea King making its way up towards the Douglas Gully. The controller on the other end of the phone confirmed they had got his message. Giving the phone back to the climber, he told them the story of what had occurred during their climb. The climbers gave Jon a lift to the Accident and Emergency Department at Belford Hospital in Fort William. Jim arrived in the helicopter at the hospital at the same time as Jon. He was suffering badly from hypothermia but it probably saved his life, because he had been bleeding in the pelvic area from the three fractures in there. Jim's core temperature was brought back to normal, then the Surgeons operated on him immediately to sort out the fractures to his pelvis, leg and left wrist.

Jon had his hand stitched back together and then went outside with his climbing gear and threw it away in the Police skip. He knew then that he would never climb again.

His pal had been brought in and Jon went to view and identify him, observing a nasty injury to his head. The post mortem would find that he had died from blood in his lungs, causing suffocation. Jon to this day, wonders if he could have saved his friend.

The two ladies had now arrived at the hospital and Jon met them to explain what had happened. He told them Jim was in theatre having his broken bones sorted out, then one asked about his pal. Jon was in a dilemma on how he was going to tell her he had died. He then took her into a side room in the hospital and broke the tragic news.

The three of them spent the next two days in Fort William visiting Jim and sorting out his pal's return home after the post mortem had been performed.

This tragedy was to haunt Jon for months, because he kept seeing his pal's face in the fleeting moment as he fell down the mountain.

Returning to work, after taking some time off for his injury to heal, Jon found the office quite empty without Jim who spent many months in hospital recovering from his injuries. Fortunately Jon had the other pilot to feed his thoughts off and as they got on with the normal rescues and work commitments, Jon made up his mind he wanted to become a Commercial Helicopter Pilot.

First thing was to obtain a Helicopter Pilot's Licence then progress from there to gain a Commercial Licence. He registered with an Instructor, Steve Hetherington, at Newcastle Airport and started his training. Jon soon got to grips with the controls and was flying the helicopter with some confidence. Over the next few months Jon flew as many times as he could during his time off to improve his ability at flying the helicopter.

It was during this time, Jon found out someone had put his name forward for a Vodafone Life Saving Award. He won the Regional Award and was then put forward for a National Award which was to be presented in London. There were lots of contenders from around the country but only ten would receive an award.

On Wednesday 1st November 2006 Jon and his partner, Barbara, were invited to London where he won a Life Saving Award. Jon was presented with his trophy for his dramatic climb and rescue on Ben Nevis. His friend Jim, now on crutches, was also there and he praised Jon for his selfless act, risking his own life to save him. The next day Jon went to number 10 Downing Street and received an accolade from the Prime Minister. It highlighted the dangerous rescue after the accident and took away some of the grief he had suffered with losing one of his best pal's during the climb.

Chapter 11: Flight to France in Helicopter

Jon's practice and determination soon helped him achieve his Helicopter Pilot's Licence. He had already planned to accompany his mates on their next microlight trip to France. Jon would hire a helicopter for the duration of the trip and Jim, who was getting around much better now, would accompany Jon for their journey. Eddie and John Hood were also on the trip with three other friends.

It was the 9th June 2007 as everyone flew down to Sandown on the Isle of Wight first, filling up with fuel before they set off across the English Channel for Cherbourg in France. It was a short flight across the channel to Cherbourg, but it was now after eight o'clock in the evening so they stayed there overnight.

At 10 30am the next morning saw them flying south to Avranches and after an hour's break they set off and flew west arriving at St. Malo just before one o'clock. After an overnight stop they travelled south towards Les Sables d'Olonne and the small Talmont Airport. They stayed at the west coast town that day and night.

During their time at the airport, Jon took his friend John Hood up in the helicopter, explaining to him how all the controls worked and showing him his skill at hovering over the same spot just above the ground.

At La Salbe de Lonne Spain with John Hood in passenger seat.

Their next destination was Arcachon further down the west coast on the Bay of Biscay. Flying straight down the coast they all arrived at Arcachon, which is just south west of Bordeaux, about two o'clock in the afternoon. The next two days were spent chilling out around Arcachon Bay and the Bordeaux area.

Setting off on the 14th June, saw the group heading north east to Chauvigny, where they landed for a short while before moving on in an easterly direction to Bourges, staying there overnight. The next day saw them flying north to Chartres which was achieved in just an hour and twenty minutes. They went into the town and relaxed having a meal and drink. At 19 15 hours they took off and flew to Abbeville arriving there in just over an hour, at the Aerodrome d'Abbeville-Drucat. They safely parked the helicopter and microlights and stayed the night.

Just before eleven the next morning, the team set off for Le Touquet Airport but due to the poor weather conditions, they aborted the journey and flew back to Abbeville. By six o'clock in the evening the weather had cleared slightly, so after filling up with fuel, they set off across the English Channel landing in Headcorn, Kent, staying the night. The group stayed at the small grassed airfield overnight.

The next day saw them all heading home with Eddie and John returning to Longframlington and Jon flying the helicopter back to Teesside Airport, from where he had hired it.

It had been a good trip but for Jon, it had also given him a lot more air miles flying the helicopter preparing him for his commercial licence.

Chapter 12: Racing the Orient Express to Istanbul

Jon's next planned challenge was to raise money for the Great North Air Ambulance by racing the Orient Express from Paris to Istanbul. The reason for raising this money was because the Great North Air Ambulance is a charity and relies on donations to keep it in the air.

The route would take them through France, Germany, Austria, Hungary, Romania and Bulgaria before finishing in Turkey. Jim, who was still on crutches, would act as navigator on the trip with Jon doing all the driving. Their vehicle would be a Fiat Panda with an automatic gearbox.

As I said to Jon, "It's a good job it's automatic, because you would soon wreck the gearbox driving flat out trying to beat the train."

The 1994 Fiat Panda had a history. It had been in several episodes of a popular television soap opera and also, during 2005, had appeared in a fast food advert on television. Its top speed was about 75 miles per hour downhill. It had been bought for £120 and was now racing a luxury train costing millions of pounds.

The challenge started on the 31st August 2007 as train and Fiat Panda moved out of the Paris railway station together. Keeping off the main roads Jon and Jim headed for the Orient Express's first stop at Strasbourg, France. The drive took all day and they reached Strasbourg late evening. Finding a small hotel they had a nightcap and prepared themselves for the next day. The train had beaten them that day so it had to be an early start on the following morning.

Starting early the pair set off for Munich in Germany. Again it was a full day driving through the countryside of Eastern France into Western Germany. Once more the train arrived first in Munich. It was going to be hard work to beat the train.

Next day saw them up at the crack of dawn heading for Vienna in Austria, the Orient Express's next destination. The roads were pretty good so they made good time as they crossed the Austrian border. It still took most of the day to reach Vienna and they were slower than the train.

The next destination was Budapest and when they crossed over into Hungary, they suddenly found the roads were worse for wear.

Jon commented, "I had to constantly watch out for potholes in the road, otherwise I would have wrecked the car because they were so deep."

Again they mainly stayed off the motorways as they made their way to Budapest. The journey wasn't too long so they were able to rest a bit and see the sights of the city.

The following day saw them heading for Bucharest in Romania, which was an extensive trip, taking them more than ten hours to complete. The roads weren't any better than in Hungary so it was a hard day's driving. The Orient Express had again arrived before them but they had a plan for the rest of the journey, which hopefully would give them an advantage of beating it.

They headed for Golden Sands in Bulgaria the next day which gave them the chance on the final day to drive straight down the coast to Sirkeci Railway Station in Istanbul. They set off really early that final day knowing it was going to be touch and go whether they beat the train into Sirkeci.

As they pulled into Sirkeci Railway Station, they encountered large crowds that had congregated around the station platforms to meet the Orient Express. It was about four in the afternoon and the pair thought, with all the crowds, the train was already in but as they pulled onto the platform, they saw it hadn't yet arrived. They had won the race and beaten the train, which arrived about thirty minutes later. They shook hands with the train driver and chatted to him about how they had managed to beat the famous train into Istanbul Railway Station. They had also made quite a substantial amount of money for the Great North Air Ambulance.

The journey home took a slightly shorter time as they used the motorways to cut across all the countries. They caught the ferry at Calais and were soon back in England, with a steady drive to Teesside Airport, where some of the staff were waiting to greet their return. The challenge had been arduous but both men had enjoyed the experience and had made some money for the charity to boot.

Jon at Paris Railway Station just before the Orient Express set off for Istanbul

Jon and Jim about to leave Paris Railway Station

Jon and Jim on the Platform at Istanbul Railway Station after beating the Orient Express

Back to work Jon started concentrating on the theory he needed to learn regarding achieving his Commercial Helicopter Pilot's Licence. He initially found it quite hard but he was able to tap into Jim's wealth of knowledge and experience, which helped immensely. As Christmas approached Jon was ready to take his Licence Assessment and he booked it at

Gatwick Airport for the first week in January. As we know, it didn't take place due to the near fatal microlight crash.

Chapter 13: Recovery after Air Crash

It was the second of January 2008 and Jon was sent for another scan on his brain. He was still in an induced coma and the fresh scan showed the bleeding had stopped and the clot in his brain was reducing, which led the Consultant to start to bring him out of the coma. He did warn us, he didn't know what damage to the brain had been realised from the bleed and only time would reveal the extent of it. He painted the grimmest picture of how Jon would be when they brought him out of the coma.

Over the next three days, Jon slowly regained full consciousness. It was on the fourth day when incredibly he looked up, recognised us and confirmed we were Barbara, Mam and Dad. It was a great relief but we knew he had a long road ahead to full recovery.

Jon's other injuries needed urgent treatment, especially his right ankle which required a skin graft because it had all been torn off during the crash. He was transferred to Royal Victoria Infirmary (RVI) Hospital in Newcastle where the skin grafts were performed successfully. The Surgeon stated there was no infection in his wounds, so the graft should heal well. However on checking his mouth during surgery, they found he had the MRSA virus, so he was placed in a side ward to isolate him from other patients.

In these early days as his leg healed we realized Jon's short term memory was not working at all. He couldn't remember we had been in to see him. We would go into the ward in the morning and when we went back again in the afternoon, he didn't know we had been in earlier that day. His friends would visit him but he couldn't tell you who had been present. It was during this time, we noticed Jon wasn't moving his left leg at all. I would tell him he had broken his left femur which had a pin in it and he must get it moving again to help the healing process. He still didn't move it, so we had a word with the Physiotherapist and they started to get him moving.

In just a week he was standing and walking with crutches, moving up and down the ward corridor. Fortunately the ward was locked but one day Jon had somehow got out of the ward and ended up at the front reception area where he was rescued by staff. On our arrival we got the full story but Jon couldn't remember a thing.

He was now being assessed for a move to the Head Trauma Hospital at Walkergate on the edge of Newcastle. Unfortunately the transfer was delayed a couple of weeks because of the MRSA. Finally he got the all clear and on 30th January 2008 he started the specialist treatment at Walkergate Hospital. In the first couple of weeks we saw some improvement, as his long term memory began to return. One thing appeared to us, Jon had lost the memory between nine and twelve of the previous months in his life. We knew because when we were getting him to recall past events, he was adamant that the accident on Ben Nevis had happened just last January, when it had actually occurred two years ago.

After a month we had a case conference with the Consultant and nursing staff regarding Jon's progress. They were pleased with him but couldn't confirm whether his short memory would recover completely and be back to where it had been prior to the accident. The Consultant stated he might not regain the full functions of his short term memory and it would take about two to three years before it can be realised how much the brain has recovered.

During our normal visits to Walkergate, there were several occasions when Jon became quite agitated and frustrated with being restricted to the Trauma Unit. He would quickly lose his temper with us for no specific reason. One of his friends witnessed this, commenting on the outburst and the way he had spoken to his mother. The same friend also thought Jon had changed in character since the accident, something we had already noticed.

One of the funniest moments during our many visits, we had been talking to Jon for about half an hour when he suddenly said he was going to the toilet. We sat there waiting for him to come back for ten, fifteen then twenty minutes. I went to see the nurse on duty and explained what had happened, she took me along to Jon's room and there he was laid on his bed watching television.

He said, "Hi Dad, I didn't know you were here."

I explained to him, "Your Mam and me were talking to you when you went to the toilet, had you forgotten we were still here."

He laughed and got up walking back to the canteen area with me, we then played cards and dominoes to help him use his short term memory. It didn't appear to cause him any distress and he just laughed off the incident. I suppose this was a good thing because he continued to make strides towards his recovery.

It was now March and Jon had remarkably improved his walking with crutches. The skin graft had healed well and with the physiotherapy, his left leg was becoming stronger. He would go to the local shops to collect papers and other things for the patients but was always accompanied by a nurse.

This culminated in him being allowed a home visit on the 13th March and then an overnight stay two days later. That short visit home caused Jon to show signs of frustration again after returning to Walkergate. When we next saw him, he would explain that everyone in there had a big problem but he didn't and felt it was time he should be allowed home for good.

Although Jon's short term memory was not improving very well, his physical side was developing rapidly, because of the regular visits to the fully equipped gymnasium at the Unit. In view of this advancement in his wellbeing Jon with two of the nurses in attendance, went to his home at Rothbury where they assessed him.

Checking he could climb the stairs safely with his crutches they walked him down into the village. To their surprise they found it really difficult keeping up with Jon even though he was on crutches. Also once on the High Street, everyone they met was stopping him and asking how he was doing. This impressed the nurses, who realised how popular the Paramedic was in Rothbury.

This visit was just before Easter and after a couple of nights back at Walkergate he was allowed to go home and spend the Easter weekend there. Two weeks later, much to his delight, on the 7th April 2008 he was finally discharged from the Trauma Unit in Newcastle. However there were follow up appointments arranged, with the Nursing Staff from Walkergate at his home, to make sure he was making progress and not reverting back into the chronic state of his arrival at the Unit.

We found the Trauma Hospital had got Jon into a regime which even today he follows to some degree. It had been put in place to help with the recovery from the brain trauma and was followed by him religiously during the next twelve months. He would be out of bed and eating his breakfast by eight o'clock, which in the past was never the case unless he was at work. Lunch was at twelve on the dot, dinner at six, then a bath at seven and back to bed between ten and half past. He had always been a late night person even when he was at school and college.

Jon's next step was to get rid of his crutches so he could walk his dogs and this was soon achieved, which again took him forward as far as his physical wellbeing was concerned. However he was slipping back regarding his mental state. We found he had lost his drive and would just sit about during the day watching television, which wasn't stimulating his brain at all. The visits by nursing staff from the hospital had stopped and he was left to his own devices. One of the funny things which used to happen was Jon would ring and tell us about something he had done that day, then about an hour later he would ring again and tell us the same thing. When we prompted him and explained he had already told us, he laughed it off and started talking about something else.

It was at this time that he received a letter from the Great North Air Ambulance (GNAA) stating his contract was terminated because he could no longer do his job. This was a gargantuan blow to Jon who was now only receiving basic disability allowance. He had always been able to work and earn a decent living but now his future looked bleak with his short term memory still very poor.

It was now nearly two years since Jon had left hospital. Physically he was in good shape considering all the injury damage to his legs. What had helped him was a training job building dry stone walls. There was a possible job at the end of it. He really enjoyed the work which built the muscles in his legs and arms during the four week tuition. Unfortunately there was no job available at the end of the course. However he continued to develop his fitness and this was evident when his friends decided they would take him for a walk over the moors near Rothbury.

As Jon said, "When we got to the top of the hill leading to the moors they were all blowing like "puffa billys" and I was quite some distance ahead of them. I think they regretted going with me. We had a good walk but they never asked me again after that."

He was desperate now to get a job and start earning some money. He was offered a job at a local Doctor's Surgery taking blood pressures and blood samples for testing. This was just right for him, as he hadn't forgotten anything regarding his Paramedic training and experience. He spent a six week probation period with the surgery but was not kept on after it had expired. At the time his short term memory was quite poor and I think this was the reason they didn't keep him on.

He then got a job at the local Golf Club serving behind the bar and other duties around the club house. He had been warned that the job only lasted during the summer period so he started looking straight away for a job where his skills could be used.

He got in touch with a firm, based in Ross-on-Wye, who were looking for Paramedics to work offshore on Survey Ships looking for oil and gas, also other worldwide medic placements which were required to be filled. I drove Jon down to Ross-on-Wye for his interview. It lasted some four hours and he was successful in getting a job. First thing though, he had to obtain certificates to practice which the firm paid for him to do. Jon soon completed the re-qualifications and in the June he joined a Survey Ship in the North Sea, working for five weeks at sea, then five weeks at home. This continued until the end of August when the North Sea was just too rough for any surveys to be done.

Chapter 14: Rocket Attack Iraq

His next contract was to Iraq and he flew out there on the 12th September 2010. His role there was to travel as the Paramedic in a convoy of vehicles, which were looking for land mines. The experts were clearing the mines in preparation for an Oil Company to start drilling for oil and gas near Basra. The convoy always went out in the same formation. The lead vehicle was a security firm, Jon was in the second vehicle, the third truck was Iraqi security with the bomb disposal guys following them and a security firm vehicle bringing up the rear.

Jon had been there for seven weeks, longer than expected, getting used to the daily schedule. He doesn't know why to this day, but as they went out on the 10th November, that particular morning he found himself in the third vehicle. The Iraqi's were in the second truck and the convoy travelled out on the usual route.

Suddenly there was an enormous explosion. Jon felt the shock waves as he sat in the rear of his vehicle. Everyone jumped out of the vehicles and saw the second vehicle in the convoy had been destroyed by a rocket launcher. As Jon ran over to it, he saw straight away that the driver had been killed instantly. However the Iraqi passenger in the vehicle was still alive but the pressure of the explosion had collapsed both his lungs. Jon quickly got his medical bag and performed chest drains which released the collapsed lungs and the Iraqi could breathe again. He was in a bad way as the ambulance arrived but still alive and very likely to recover from the blast.

Jon said, "I managed to stabilize him and get him ready for the ambulance. When the ambulance arrived, the medics put him on a stretcher and as I turned to pick up my medical bag to go with the Iraqi to hospital, the ambulance drove off at high speed, leaving me quite flabbergasted among the wreckage. Apparently that's what happens here in Iraq."

The convoy returned to their compound and they never went out again while Jon was in Iraq. He was commended for his quick and decisive action in saving the life of the Iraqi. The security firm also offered him a permanent job straight away at a massive salary but after some quick thought and reflection he turned it down. The dangers were too great and the money didn't cover it.

Another near miss, another of his nine lives used up!!

Convoy Vehicle which was blown up in Iraq

His next contract saw him back onboard ship and sailing to Singapore. Five weeks later, as the survey boat completed the work, it sailed into Mumbai in India. Once the passports and visas had been sorted out Jon flew home. He returned to Mumbai five weeks later for the next crew change and the ship left port, heading for Egypt. As he finished his next stint of five weeks in Egyptian waters, Jon was offered a permanent job on the Shetland Isles working in the Oil fields.

He only stayed for a month because the firm involved had broken every promise they had made regarding the duties of the four medics who had been employed. All but one left within the month and Jon returned to the survey boat in Egypt for the normal crew change. Fortunately he hadn't resigned from his previous firm and was glad to be back with the ship. The next port of call was a sea journey to Vana in Bulgaria, through the Aegean Sea, the Sea of Marmara and into the Black Sea.

Chapter 15: Held at Gunpoint Iran

On finishing the survey in the Black Sea the ship sailed to Cyprus for the five week crew change. Jon took his leave and returned five weeks later to Dubai and then to Shasha Sharjah where the boat was berthed. They sailed into the Persian Gulf on the second day but had only been under way for four hours, when the Party Chief appeared to be having a heart attack. Jon had limited resources to treat him but kept him comfortable, managing to get some painkillers to ease the pain as the ship turned around and headed back to port. An Ambulance was waiting as they tied up on the dockside and the Party Chief was taken straight to hospital. He had attended the same hospital, the previous day to their departure, with chest pains but the Doctors had told him it was only indigestion. He was operated on straight away and a stent was put into the blocked artery in his heart. The next day saw him back on board and he thanked Jon for his care during the heart attack.

The boat again set sail into the Persian Gulf and started laying the tracers to try and discover if there was any oil and gas present on the sea bed. It was during this time that the next life threatening incident occurred. It was the 4th May 2012 and the ship was sailing back towards Sharjah from Iran, having completed the survey. They were now in the Strait of Hormuz and International waters, when an Iranian Navy Gun Boat pulled alongside the Survey Ship.

The armed Navy sailors boarded the ship immediately and herded everyone at gunpoint, onto the ship's helicopter pad. As Jon arrived on the deck, a uniformed sailor prodded a loaded cocked pistol into his temple. Another Survey crew member had a semiautomatic rifle driven into his stomach. The captain was then ordered to sail his ship to Iran and the crew, with Jon, were detained on the helicopter deck at gunpoint all the way to the Iranian Port of Bandi Abas.

Jon had managed to get a message to Barbara and she made contact with his company to find out what was happening about the hijack of the survey ship. The company were very good at keeping us informed concerning what was happening with the ship and its crew. They were finally released after being held for three days in Iran.

On returning home Jon stated, "It was pretty scary especially when that loaded gun was shoved in my temple. I could see the safety catch was off and he kept me in that position for a long time."

Jon was well relieved when his next contract was on another ship owned by a different firm.

Chapter 16: Life Goes On

Jon is enjoying his present job working five weeks on board and then five weeks off. He is seeing different parts of the world, visiting the Falkland Islands recently, then back up to the Norwegian coast. He has also been to Kenya, Tanzania, Congo, Senegal and Cote D'Ivoire (Ivory Coast) besides Iraq, Iran, India, Egypt, Cyprus, United Arab Emirates, Bulgaria and Singapore that I've already mentioned .

He relates one story on board the ship saying, "We were at Mumbai in India and intending to sail to the Black sea but it meant going through the Suez Canal and past Somalia on the way to it. It was decided because the threat of pirates attacking the ship, that only the marine crew would stay on board and of course me. We had four security guards put on board, all ex marines who razor wired the whole ship and when we approached Somalia they locked us down in a secure room in the ship. Fortunately we weren't attacked but it was worrying knowing that it could easily happen."

His quest, to some degree, for excitement still goes on but not to the same intensity as it was before his near fatal accident.

His life goes on and considering the serious head injury he received in the crash, his short term memory and loss of smell, are the only permanent damages he appears to have incurred. However, his short memory appears to be improving. The thought of one Consultant Neurologist is that the brain will continue to improve for about ten years but apparently, like muscles, it needs to be exercised regularly.

He has had further surgery on his legs to remove the screws and plate in his right ankle and also to remove the screw holding the femur rod just above his knee. The reason for the metal being taken away was because he had a lot of pain at the site of each injury, caused by the protrusions of the bolts and plates.

The loss of smell however, can be a dangerous thing. One day when he was at home Jon had put the oven on to cook the tea but he had failed to notice a wooden spoon in the back of the oven. Babs returned from work and was able to smell the burning wood straight away as she entered the house. The smoke was just starting to develop and they quickly retrieved the spoon from the oven thus averting a fire. Jon hadn't smelt a thing but fortunately Babs had returned just in time or there might have been a serious blaze.

He manages to keep fit on board ship by walking round the helipad many times each day which keeps the muscles in his legs strong. There is also a well equipped gymnasium on board. He still has some wastage in his left leg where the metal pin was in the femur. A physiotherapist has given him some exercises to improve the vastus medialis muscle, which is located just above the knee and aides with the final ten per cent of leg extension. When Jon is at home he takes their dogs out twice a day onto the moor top near Rothbury, maintaining the strength in his legs.

We are hoping all his mishaps are a thing of the past but guess what, when he went on holiday with Barbara to New York, Hurricane Sandy showed up just as they were about to fly home. They were confined to the hotel and Jon described how everything in the "Big Apple" ground to a halt. Virtually the whole of the next week kept them inside the hotel, with nothing moving in or out of the city. They finally got the all clear and flew home, but the extra week cost him a lot more money, even though it wasn't his fault.

One thing that hasn't changed is Jon's sense of humour. It has no doubt helped him during his recovery period. It must have been frustrating, not being able to remember what has happened just hours earlier in the day, but he was able to laugh about it and didn't get disheartened. His friends John and Eddie, certainly provided the mirth and frivolity on their visits to the hospital and the Head Trauma Unit. Another thing he loves doing is finding funny articles and posting them on facebook, with his many friends sending him some as well.

He can also laugh at himself, telling the story of when he was on Huayna Potosi in Bolivia. They were about halfway up having a rest, when he saw the sherpas, who were with them, having a smoke. So he thought I'll have one, if they can smoke up here so can I. How wrong he was, within minutes he had a blinding headache and had to lay down for over half an hour, until the effects of the cigarette went away.

Four years after the plane crash Jon and Jim were finally awarded compensation for their injuries by a Judge at Newcastle Crown Court. Unfortunately they haven't received a penny to this day. The Judge praised both men for not sitting about waiting for compensation but getting on with their lives and finding work, when they could have been on the scrap heap.

During one of his downtimes, Jon flew to Bucharest, Romania to visit his friend Jim. Whilst there Jim had introduced him to a helicopter flying instructor. After having a long chat with the guy, he ended up flying one of the helicopters, trying the hover to see if he could still do it. That zest for life is still there.

Another change in his life appears to be his body clock. Jon was always a late bird, even as a child he would be awake late into the evening. This is not the case anymore, because as soon as ten o'clock at night comes around, he's ready for his bed.

I think one disappointment for Jon is, he never got to climb in the Himalayan Mountains, especially up Everest. He had been asked to go on an expedition there, as the medic, but it never materialised for whatever reason. However Jon did achieve a couple of other things, one was the race up Kirkstone Pass in the Lake District, pulling a car which weighed one ton, from Ambleside to the Kirkstone Pass Inn at the top. His team on the day recorded the fastest time ever for the run. However, a rugby team, who competed two hours later, were able to beat their time.

The other achievement was climbing the three highest peaks in the United Kingdom, which are Ben Nevis, ScaFell Pike and Snowdon within twenty four hours. The event was for charity and called the "Emergency Services Challenge." Police, Fire and Ambulance teams all participated. Jon and a team from the Ambulance Service took part, which was during his time as a Paramedic at Rothbury. They all started to climb Ben Nevis but Jon with two others, decided to climb Tower Ridge to the top of the "Ben" whilst the rest of the team walked up the normal track. This delayed their schedule, in continuing to the Lake District to climb Scafell Pike, so this climb was completed overnight. They then travelled to Snowdon and started climbing early in the morning. However the two guys who had gone up Tower Ridge with Jon were unable to climb Snowdon because of fatigue. He reached the top in just under the twenty four hours.

One thing that has been said, a bit tongue in cheek, is that Jon and Jim are not allowed to go out together or on anymore adventures because of their track record of getting into trouble.

December 2013 saw the twenty fifth anniversary of the Lockerbie bombing and I think it is a thing that is never far away from Jon's thoughts. In the October when he was home, he made a trip to Lockerbie village.

Jon explained to me, "It was weird Dad!! as I drove into the village, all the memories came flooding back, it was a strange feeling. I went into the cemetery and saw the Memorial Wall, such a peaceful setting - I'm glad I went back and remembered."